TRAVEL GUIDE TO TALLINN 2023

A Budget-Friendly Insider's Guide To Unconventional Activities And Points of Interest Beyond The Tourist Trail. Uncovering the City's Culture, Cuisine and History

By

DWAYNE WATERMAN

@COPYRIGHT 2023 BY DWAYNE WATERMAN
ALL RIGHTS RESERVED.

Contents

INTRODUCTION...5

CHAPTER 1: GETTING TO KNOW TALLINN 8

Getting to Know Tallinn: A Brief Introduction to Estonia's Capital...12

CHAPTER 2: TOP 10 MUST-SEE SIGHTS IN TALLINN: FROM MEDIEVAL OLD TOWN TO THE MODERN CITY 16

CHAPTER 3: HIDDEN GEMS: OFF-THE-BEATEN-PATH PLACES TO EXPLORE IN TALLINN...20

CHAPTER 4: TALLINN'S LOCAL RESTAURANTS & ESTONIAN CUISINE: A FOODIE'S GUIDE 28

CHAPTER 5: DAY TRIPS FROM TALLINN: EXPLORING ESTONIA'S COUNTRYSIDE AND COASTAL TOWNS.................................42

The Various Costs Associated With Visiting Estonia's Coastal Towns And Countryside 46

CHAPTER 6: TALLINN ON A BUDGET: HOW TO EXPERIENCE THE CITY WITHOUT BREAKING THE BANK 52

CHAPTER 7: TALLINN FOR FAMILIES: FUN ACTIVITIES AND ATTRACTIONS FOR KIDS AND PARENTS ALIKE 73

CHAPTER 8: NIGHTLIFE IN TALLINN: THE BEST BARS, CLUBS, AND VENUES TO CHECK OUT AFTER DARK 84

CHAPTER 9: EXPLORING TALLINN'S CULTURAL SCENE: MUSEUMS, GALLERIES, AND PERFORMING ARTS VENUES 91

CHAPTER 10: ACTIVE ADVENTURES IN TALLINN: HIKING, BIKING, AND WATER SPORTS IN AND AROUND THE CITY 100

CHAPTER 11: WHERE TO STAY IN TALLINN: FROM LUXURY HOTELS TO BUDGET HOSTELS AND APARTMENTS 107

CHAPTER 12: SEASONAL EVENTS IN TALLINN: FESTIVALS, MARKETS, AND CELEBRATIONS THROUGHOUT THE YEAR 119

CHAPTER 13: DISCOVERING TALLINN'S SOVIET PAST: EXPLORING THE CITY'S HISTORY AND ARCHITECTURE................................127

CHAPTER 14: PLANNING YOUR TRIP TO TALLINN: TIPS ON VISAS, TRANSPORTATION, AND LOCAL CUSTOMS.............................132

CONCLUSION 137

INTRODUCTION

Tallinn, the capital of Estonia, is a beautiful and historic city that offers visitors an abundance of cultural, historical, and natural attractions. The city's well-preserved Old Town is a UNESCO World Heritage site, and it has a long history that dates back to the medieval period. Whether you are interested in exploring the city's historical landmarks, dining on local cuisine, or experiencing the vibrant nightlife, Tallinn has something to offer everyone.

If you are planning a trip to Tallinn, it's important to know what to expect regarding weather, events, and activities. Tallinn is best experienced during the summer months of June, July, and August when the sun shines brightly, and there are several outdoor activities to partake in. However, the summer season is also the busiest for tourists, so you should anticipate a lot of people and greater costs.

Consider visiting Tallinn in May, September, or October during the shoulder seasons if you want a more sedate and budget-friendly experience. The city is less busy, and the weather is still beautiful throughout these months, making it simpler to explore the city's sites and attractions. You can also find some great deals on accommodations during this time.

When planning your trip to Tallinn, consider the length of your stay and your interests. A weekend trip is enough to explore the Old Town and some of the city's other highlights, but if you want to explore the surrounding areas and take day trips, you may want to stay for a week or longer. The city is easily walkable, and many of its attractions are within walking distance, but you may consider renting a bicycle or using public transportation.

There are many possibilities for lodging to match every price range and inclination. While the neighboring districts provide more up-to-date and reasonably priced lodging choices, the Old Town is home to a selection of lovely and historic hotels. Additionally, you can locate guesthouses, hostels, and rental flats.

Planning ahead and learning about the city's attractions and events are crucial for making the most of your vacation to Tallinn. The Tallinn Card is recommended since it allows you to use the city's public transit system for free and grants you free or cheap admission to many of the city's museums and attractions. Additionally, you may benefit from the free walking tours provided by neighborhood guides, which give a wonderful introduction to the history and culture of the city.

In summary, Tallinn is a charming and ancient city that offers tourists a distinctive fusion of culture, history, and natural beauty. There is something for everyone in Tallinn, whether you want to see the city's attractions, sample the food, or partake in the lively nightlife. Make the most of your time away and collect experiences that will last a lifetime with little advanced preparation and study.

CHAPTER 1: GETTING TO KNOW TALLINN

Estonia's capital city, Tallinn, is situated on the Baltic Sea coast in the country's northern region. With a population of around 450,000 people, it is the largest city in Estonia and one of the region's most important economic and cultural centers. The city is known for its beautiful medieval Old Town, a UNESCO World Heritage site, as well as its modern architecture, vibrant cultural scene, and excellent cuisine.

Tallinn is easily accessible by air, with direct flights from many major European cities and by ferry from Helsinki, Stockholm, and St. Petersburg. Buses, trams, and trolleybuses link all areas of the city as part of the well-developed public transportation infrastructure in the city. There are also many taxis and ride-sharing options available.

From luxurious hotels to inexpensive hostels, Tallinn offers a variety of lodging choices for travelers. There are also numerous restaurants, cafes, bars, nightclubs, museums, galleries, and theaters. The city is a popular destination for business and leisure travelers, offering a rich and diverse cultural experience.

History of Tallinn

Tallinn's long and rich history dates back to the early Middle Ages. German traders who built a trading station on the site of an earlier Estonian hamlet in the 13th century are credited with founding the city. Over the centuries, Tallinn grew and developed into a major center of commerce and culture, attracting merchants, craftsmen, and artists from Europe.

During the medieval period, Tallinn was one of the most important cities in the Baltic region, and its Old Town is a testament to this era. A peek into medieval life is provided by the city's well-preserved walls, towers, and structures, which date to the 14th and 15th centuries.

In the 16th and 17th centuries, Tallinn came under the control of the Swedish Empire, and it remained a part of Sweden until the early 18th century. During this time, the city continued to thrive, and many of its most iconic buildings, including the town hall and St. Olaf's Church, were constructed.

Tallinn was annexed to Russia in the 18th and 19th centuries and remained a part of the country until the early 20th century.

The city underwent significant modernization during this time, with new buildings, parks, and infrastructure projects. However, it was also a time of political unrest and social upheaval as Estonians struggled for independence and autonomy.

In the 20th century, Tallinn was caught up in the tumultuous events of World War II and the subsequent Soviet occupation. However, the city has seen a rebirth as a result of fresh investments in infrastructure, tourism, and culture after Estonia reclaimed its independence in 1991.

Geography of Tallinn

The Estonian capital of Tallinn is on the Gulf of Finland, in the country's northernmost region. The city covers an area of around 159 square kilometers, and it is divided into eight administrative districts. The landscape around Tallinn is characterized by rolling hills, forests, and lakes, and the city is home to several large parks and green spaces.

Tallinn has a humid continental climate, with warm summers (about 20 degrees Celsius) and frigid winters (as low as minus 20 degrees Celsius). Snowfall is common during winter, and the city is known for its beautiful winter landscapes.

Tallinn is a port city with a well-developed harbor that connects it to the rest of the world. The port is the largest in Estonia and is a hub for shipping, trade, and transportation. The city also has a major international airport, the Lennart Meri Tallinn Airport, which offers direct flights to many major European cities.

In terms of transportation, Tallinn has an extensive network of buses, trams, and trolleybuses that provide affordable and convenient access to all parts of the city. The city also has a well-developed cycling infrastructure, with bike lanes and paths that make it easy to get around on two wheels.

Culture of Tallinn

Tallinn has a rich and diverse cultural scene, a vibrant arts community, a thriving music scene, and a strong tradition of storytelling and literature. The city has several cultural events and festivals all year long, and it is also home to numerous museums, art galleries, and theaters.

The Old Town in Tallinn, which is one of the city's most recognizable cultural icons and is a UNESCO World Heritage site, is home to several historic structures, churches, and museums. The town hall, which dates back to the 14th century, is one of the city's most impressive examples of medieval architecture.

Another important cultural institution in Tallinn is the Estonian National Opera, which hosts various operas, ballet, and other performances throughout the year. The theater is situated in a gorgeous edifice from the early 20th century and is a well-liked attraction for both residents and tourists.

In addition to the arts, Tallinn is also known for its cuisine, which features many traditional Estonian dishes and international cuisine. There is a wide variety of eateries in the city, from quick eats to five-star restaurants.

Finally, Tallinn is a city deeply rooted in tradition and folklore. Many of the city's festivals and cultural events are centered around traditional Estonian customs and practices, such as the midsummer festival of Jaanipäev and the Christmas traditions of Jõulud. The city is also home to many storytellers and musicians who keep the rich heritage of Estonian culture and history alive.

Getting to Know Tallinn: A Brief Introduction to Estonia's Capital.

Tallinn, the capital city of Estonia, is a stunningly beautiful destination that has recently gained immense popularity among travelers worldwide. Located on the southern shore of the Gulf of Finland, the historic city of Tallinn charms visitors with its fascinating fusion of ancient and contemporary culture.

The city's rich history dates back to the 13th century when it was first established as a trading hub for the Hanseatic League. Throughout the centuries, various foreign powers, including Denmark, Sweden, and Russia, occupied Tallinn. The city's architecture, food, and customs now reflect the wide range of people who have lived there throughout the years.

Tallinn's medieval old town is one of the best-preserved in Europe and one of the city's most stunning characteristics. The ancient town's stunning architecture, cobblestone walkways, and winding alleys have earned it a spot on the UNESCO World Heritage list.

Visitors can explore the town's historical landmarks, including the imposing Toompea Castle, the Gothic St. Mary's Cathedral, and the Town Hall Square, home to the famous Tallinn Christmas Market.

Tallinn is home to both a historic district and a bustling contemporary city center, both of which are worth seeing. The city's main shopping street, Viru Street, is lined with trendy boutiques and cafes, while the nearby Telliskivi Creative City is a hub for artists, designers, and creatives.

For those interested in cultural experiences, Tallinn has a vibrant arts scene that includes museums, galleries, and performing arts venues. The Kumu Art Museum, which has a collection of modern and contemporary art from Estonia, is a popular destination. The Estonian National Opera and Ballet is also worth a visit, as it offers a range of world-class performances throughout the year.

Tallinn is also a great destination for foodies, as the city has a diverse culinary scene that features traditional Estonian cuisine and international dishes. Visitors can sample local specialties such as black bread, smoked fish, and the popular dessert kohuke. The city's top restaurants include NOA, which offers breathtaking views of the Gulf of Finland, and Rataskaevu 16, a cozy restaurant that serves traditional Estonian dishes.

When it comes to accommodation, Tallinn has a range of options to suit every budget. The city has several luxury hotels, such as the Telegraaf Hotel and the Hilton Tallinn Park, as well as budget-friendly hostels and apartments. The ancient town, Kadriorg, and the hip Kalamaja quarter are among the greatest places to stay.

Buses, trams, and trolleybuses all contribute to Tallinn's efficient public transit network. The city is extremely accommodating to cyclists, with a system of bike lanes that makes getting about on two wheels a breeze. Visitors can also use the city's taxi and ride-sharing services, such as Bolt and Uber.

Overall, Tallinn is a city that offers something for everyone. Whether you're interested in history, culture, food, or modern entertainment, Tallinn is a destination that will delight and inspire. With its stunning architecture, charming streets, and vibrant energy, Tallinn is a must-visit destination that should be on every traveler's list.

CHAPTER 2: TOP 10 MUST-SEE SIGHTS IN TALLINN: FROM MEDIEVAL OLD TOWN TO THE MODERN CITY

Tourists looking for a blend of ancient and contemporary cultures can consider visiting Estonia's capital, Tallinn. The city has a rich heritage that dates back to the Middle Ages and is reflected in its stunning architecture, vibrant arts scene, and unique culinary offerings. Here are the top 10 must-see sights in Tallinn that every visitor should add to their itinerary.

1.   Toompea Castle

Toompea Castle is an imposing structure that overlooks Tallinn's medieval old town. The castle has served as the seat of power for Estonia's ruling elite for centuries and is currently home to the country's parliament. Visitors can explore the castle's stunning interior, which includes the impressive Knights' Hall and the stately Assembly Hall.

2.   St. Mary's Cathedral

St. Mary's Cathedral is a Gothic masterpiece that dates back to the 13th century. The cathedral has a rich history that includes serving as the coronation site for Estonia's rulers during the Middle Ages. Visitors can admire the cathedral's striking architecture, including its soaring arches and intricate stone carvings.

3.   Town Hall Square

Town Hall Square is the heart of Tallinn's medieval old town and is home to a number of historic buildings, including the city's Town Hall and the imposing St. Nicholas' Church. Visitors can soak up the atmosphere of the square, which is surrounded by charming cafes and restaurants.

4.   Kiek in de Kök

Kiek in de Kök is a medieval tower that was once part of Tallinn's fortifications. The tower offers visitors stunning views of the city and is home to a museum that showcases Tallinn's military history. Visitors can also explore the underground tunnels that once served as part of the city's defense system.

5.   Tallinn Town Wall

The Tallinn Town Wall is one of the best-preserved medieval fortifications in Europe and offers visitors a glimpse into the city's past. Visitors can walk along the wall and admire its striking towers and gates, including the iconic Viru Gate.

6.   Kadriorg Palace and Park

Kadriorg Palace and Park is a stunning 18th-century palace that was built for Russian Empress Catherine I. The palace is surrounded by lush gardens and is home to the Estonian Art Museum's foreign art collection. Visitors can admire the palace's elegant interior and stroll through the picturesque park.

7.   Estonian Open-Air Museum

The Estonian Open-Air Museum is a fascinating outdoor museum that showcases Estonia's rural life during the 18th and 19th centuries. Visitors can explore the museum's traditional farmhouses, windmills, and churches and learn about Estonia's rich cultural heritage.

8.   Telliskivi Creative City

Telliskivi Creative City is a hip neighborhood with a thriving art and cultural community. The district is filled with artists' studios, galleries, and creative spaces and hosts a number of events and festivals throughout the year.

9.   Lennusadam Seaplane Harbour

The Lennusadam Seaplane Harbour is a unique maritime museum that is housed in a former seaplane hangar. The museum showcases Estonia's rich maritime history and features a range of interactive exhibits, including a submarine and a seaplane.

10.   Kumu Art Museum

One of the biggest and most outstanding art museums in the Baltics is the Kumu Art Museum. Along with a variety of temporary exhibits, the museum has a collection of Estonian artwork from the 18th century to the current day. Visitors can admire works by some of Estonia's most celebrated artists, including Konrad Mägi and Eduard Wiiralt.

In conclusion, Tallinn is a city with a dynamic contemporary edge and a rich history and culture. These top 10 must-see sights offer visitors a glimpse into the city's past and present, from its medieval fortifications and Gothic cathedrals to its trendy arts and culture scene.

Whether you're interested in history, art, or just soaking up the atmosphere of a new city, there's something for everyone in Tallinn. Tallinn is a city that is likely to make an impact on tourists with its magnificent architecture, lovely parks, and distinctive cultural activities. Therefore, be sure to include these top 10 attractions on your schedule for Tallinn and get ready for a memorable trip to Estonia's interior.

CHAPTER 3: HIDDEN GEMS: OFF-THE-BEATEN-PATH PLACES TO EXPLORE IN TALLINN

Tourists from all over the globe enjoy visiting Estonia's capital city, Tallinn. Anyone visiting Tallinn should be sure to explore the picturesque Old Town, which is a UNESCO World Heritage Site and home to medieval buildings and meandering cobblestone alleyways. However, there are a lot of undiscovered treasures just waiting to be discovered outside of the Old Town's well-traveled trail. We'll look at several off-the-beaten-path locations to visit in Tallinn in this post.

1. Kalamaja

The stylish, developing district of Kalamaja, which is just a short stroll from the Old Town, is where musicians, painters, and other creative types call home. The wooden buildings and industrial architecture of this once-run-down neighborhood have been rehabilitated in recent years to accommodate chic cafés, boutique stores, and street art. Visit the Telliskivi Creative City, a former manufacturing complex that has been transformed into a center for creative enterprises and events, or take a walk around the neighborhood and discover its secret courtyards and alleyways.

2. Kadriorg Park

Kadriorg Park is a sizable park that can be found close to the city's core. Early in the 18th century, Peter the Great built it as a summer retreat for the Russian imperial family. In addition to the stunning Kadriorg Palace, the park is also home to a number of museums, including the Kumu Art Museum and the Kadriorg Art Museum. The park is the ideal spot to get away from the bustle of the city since it also has formal gardens, ponds, and walking pathways.

3. Patarei Prison

For a glimpse into Estonia's darker history, head to the Patarei Prison. From the 19th century until 2004, this old jail was in operation and was infamous for its harsh surroundings and cruel treatment of inmates. Today, the jail is a museum that is available to the public, and visitors may take guided tours through the spooky and gloomy hallways. Anyone interested in Estonia's history should go there since it serves as a sobering reminder of the country's dark past.

4. Stroomi Beach

While Stroomi Beach is a terrific place to enjoy the sun and the Baltic Sea, Tallinn may not be renowned for its beaches. The beach, which is situated in the Pelguranna neighborhood, is a favorite hangout for both residents and tourists. Along with a length of sand, it has facilities including restrooms, showers, and eateries. The beach also serves as a venue for summertime activities, including outdoor film screenings and beach volleyball competitions.

5. Kumu Art Museum

The Kumu Art Museum is Estonia's biggest museum of art, and it is situated in Kadriorg Park. It hosts worldwide contemporary art exhibits as well as a collection of Estonian artwork from the 18th century to the present. The museum's architecture is particularly noteworthy, with its contemporary style offering a startling contrast to the old structures in the park nearby.

6. Nõmme

Located on the outskirts of Tallinn, Nõmme is a peaceful and picturesque neighborhood that's a world away from the hustle and bustle of the city center. Nõmme, renowned for its lovely parks and gardens, is a wonderful location to take a leisurely walk and take in Estonia's natural beauty. Don't forget to visit the Nmme Market, a charming indoor market that's a terrific location to buy regional goods and mementos.

7. Pikk Hermann Tower

Tallinn's Pikk Hermann Tower, which is prominently situated on Toompea Hill's edge, is among the city's most well-known monuments. The Estonian Parliament is housed in the tower, which is a component of the Toompea Castle complex. Visitors may ascend the steps to the top of the tower for a breathtaking view of the city and the Baltic Sea, even if the castle itself is not accessible to the general public.

8. Nõmme Snow Park

The Nmme Snow Park is a terrific place for fans of winter sports, even though Tallinn may not be well-known for its skiing and snowboarding. The park, which is situated in the Nmme neighborhood, has a number of ski runs and snowboarding jumps in addition to a tubing hill and a children's snow play area. It's a fantastic location for outdoor workouts and wintertime enjoyment.

9. Linnahall

Linnahall is a music and sports arena from the Soviet period that is situated on the outskirts of Tallinn's waterfront. Even though the structure is no longer in service, it remains a beautiful example of architecture and is worth seeing. Urban explorers and photographers like to visit this skyscraper because of its brutalist appeal and concrete façade and opulence inside.

10. Telliskivi Creative City

The Telliskivi Creative City is a former manufacturing complex that has been transformed into a center for creative firms and events. It is situated in the Kalamaja area. In addition to a market that happens every Saturday, the complex is home to a variety of cafés, stores, and art galleries. It's a terrific venue to meet some of the creatives and businesspeople in Tallinn and get a feel for the city's creative environment.

11. Rocca al Mare Open Air Museum

The Rocca al Mare, Open Air Museum, is a living history museum that depicts conventional Estonian country life. It is situated outside of Tallinn. The museum is situated in a magnificent seaside setting and has a variety of old structures, such as farmhouses, windmills, and a village church. Visitors may take part in classes and demonstrations of traditional crafts, visit the buildings, and learn about Estonia's rural heritage.

12. Kalamaja Cemetery

The Kalamaja Cemetery is a unique and intriguing location, despite the fact that it may seem odd to put a cemetery on a list of off-the-beaten-path locations to visit. Many renowned Estonians, including authors, artists, and politicians, are buried at the cemetery. Because of the exquisite sculptures and artwork that decorate the graves, it is a serene and reflective place to visit.

13. Kalarand Beach

A hidden treasure, Kalarand Beach, is situated just outside of the city of Tallinn. A day of sun, sand, and water at the beach is the ideal way to unwind after being busy in the city. In addition to relaxing on the beach and soaking up the sun, visitors may swim in the Baltic Sea.

14. Kardiorg Park

A stunning park called Kardiorg Park can be found not far from the heart of Tallinn. Beautiful gardens, water features, and sculptures can be seen in the park, which also houses a number of galleries and institutions, including the Kadriorg Art Museum and the Kumu Art Museum.

15. Botanical Gardens

The Tallinn Botanical Gardens is a hidden oasis located just outside the city center. The gardens have a variety of international plants and flowers in addition to various greenhouses that contain exotic species. The gardens are open for visitors to meander slowly around while taking in the tranquil atmosphere.

16. Epping Tower

In the historic district of Tallinn, there lies a jewel called Epping Tower. Visitors may enjoy breathtaking views of

Tallinn's skyline from the tower, one of the less well-known medieval structures in the city. The inside of the tower, which features a variety of historical displays about Tallinn, is also open to visitors.

17. Pelgulinn District

A lovely neighborhood called Pelgulinn may be found just outside the city center of Tallinn. The neighborhood is renowned for its bright wooden homes, boutiques, and neighborhood cafés and eateries. Visitors may wander around the neighborhood's peaceful streets and observe local life.

18. Kumu Roof Garden

The roof garden of the Kumu Art Museum is a secret haven situated above the museum's contemporary wing. The garden is the ideal spot to unwind and take in the breathtaking beauty of the city and provides breathtaking views of Tallinn's skyline. The museum's café provides delectable Estonian food, and visitors are welcome to stop by for a beverage or snack.

19. St. Catherine's Passage

In Tallinn's old town, there is a secret passage known as St. Catherine's Passage. The alleyway is lined with studios and workshops where regional craftspeople produce and market their goods. Visitors may buy one-of-a-kind souvenirs and observe glassblowers, jewelers, and other artisans at work on their masterpieces.

20. Maarjamäe Memorial

The Maarjamäe Memorial is a hidden gem not far from Tallinn's city center. The monument, which honors Estonia's past and present, has a variety of exhibits, including a museum devoted to Estonian history, a park with sculptures and installations, and a Soviet-era flat that provides a window into life under Soviet rule.

Finally, Tallinn is a city brimming with undiscovered treasures just waiting to be discovered. Everyone may find something to enjoy in this picturesque city of the Baltics, which offers everything from hip areas like Kalamaja to serene parks like Kadriorg. So when you visit Tallinn again, be sure to go off the main track and find some of the city's lesser-known gems.

CHAPTER 4: TALLINN'S LOCAL RESTAURANTS & ESTONIAN CUISINE: A FOODIE'S GUIDE

The history and topography of Tallinn, the capital of Estonia, have a significant impact on the city's unique culinary heritage. Estonian food is known for its simplicity, seasonal ingredient utilization, and generational transmission of traditional cooking techniques. Every eater will find something to enjoy in Tallinn, from substantial stews to delectable pastries. We'll discover the many cuisines that Tallinn has to offer while taking you on a tour of the greatest neighborhood restaurants.

1. Kohvik Must Puudel

In the center of Tallinn's Old Town, you may find the quaint café Kohvik Must Puudel. The café offers a laid-back and welcoming environment and is furnished with old items. All of the sandwiches, salads, and pastries on the menu are produced using fresh, regionally sourced ingredients. A variety of teas, coffees, and wines are also available in the café.

Price range: €5-€15

2. Kompressor

Popular pancake restaurant Kompressor offers up scrumptious and full pancakes that are ideal for a fast lunch or a satisfying meal. The pancakes are offered in both savory and sweet varieties, and they may be topped with berries, cheese, ham, or mushrooms. Kompressor is a fantastic choice for frugal tourists because of its generous quantities and affordable costs.

Price range: €5-€10

3. Rataskaevu 16

The small eatery Rataskaevu 16 offers traditional Estonian fare. Elk meatballs, pickled herring, and smoked pig chops are just a few of the menu items produced using fresh, regional ingredients. Wooden tables and exposed brick walls give the eatery a pleasant and rustic ambiance. Compared to some of the other restaurants on our list, the costs are a little higher, but the excellent cuisine and enjoyable eating experience make up for it.

Price range: €20-€40

4. F-Hoone

In Tallinn's Kalamaja neighborhood sits the hip eatery F-Hoone. The restaurant is located in a former factory and boasts a trendy and cozy industrial chic interior design. Burgers, salads, and spaghetti are just a few of the foods on the menu that are all crafted using fresh, regional ingredients. To go along with your meal, F-Hoone also provides a fantastic assortment of beers and wines.

Price range: €10-€20

5. Vanaema Juures

Traditional Estonian eatery Vanaema Juures offers filling and delicious home-cooked dishes. Meatballs, sauerkraut, and smoked salmon are just a few of the foods on the menu that are prepared using traditional family methods. With hardwood tables and chairs and a fireplace to keep you warm on winter evenings, the restaurant provides a warm and inviting ambiance.

Price range: €15-€25

6. Cafe Werner

The beautiful café known as Cafe Werner is situated in Tallinn's Kadriorg neighborhood. You may savor your lunch while admiring the magnificent surroundings on the café's charming outside patio. All of the sandwiches, salads, and pastries on the menu are produced using fresh, regionally sourced ingredients. A wonderful assortment of teas, coffees, and a few wines are also available at Cafe Werner.

Price range: €5-€15

7. Leib Resto ja Aed

In the Kalamaja neighborhood of Tallinn, there is a farm-to-table restaurant called Leib Resto ja Aed. The menu varies seasonally to match the availability of products, and the restaurant purchases all of its ingredients from nearby farmers and producers. Wooden tables and exposed brick walls give the eatery a pleasant, rustic feel. The menu offers meals crafted with fresh and regional ingredients, like lamb chops, grilled octopus, and beetroot risotto. Although the costs are a little more than at some of the other restaurants on our list, the exceptional quality of the cuisine and dedication to sustainability make the extra money well spent.

Price range: €25-€50

8. Põhjaka Manor

In a manor home that has been restored in the countryside outside of Tallinn, there is a delightful restaurant called

Phjaka Manor. With a focus on using fresh, regional foods, the restaurant provides traditional Estonian fare, such as roast beef, mushroom soup, and smoked salmon. The restaurant also has its own herb garden, and many of its meals use herbs and flowers. Although the costs are more than average, the exceptional caliber of the meal and the lovely location makes it a fantastic choice for a special event.

Price range: €30-€60

9. Boheem

In the Tallinn neighborhood of Kalamaja, there is a charming café called Boheem. The café's old decor and mismatched furnishings provide a cozy and calm ambiance. All of the sandwiches, salads, and pastries on the menu are produced using fresh, regionally sourced ingredients. Along with a limited range of beers and wines, Boheem also offers a fantastic assortment of teas and coffees.

Price range: €5-€15

10. Tchaikovsky

High-end restaurant Tchaikovsky is housed in the opulent Telegraaf Hotel in Tallinn's Old Town. The restaurant offers meals produced with the best ingredients, like beef stroganoff, foie gras, and caviar. It also serves European and Russian cuisine. With crystal chandeliers and luxurious velvet seats, the restaurant boasts an upscale and classy ambiance. Although the costs are more than average, the exceptional quality of the cuisine and the opulent eating experience make it worthwhile.

Price range: €50-€100

11. Kohvik Sesoon

The inviting café Kohvik Sesoon is situated in Tallinn's hip Telliskivi Creative City neighborhood. The café uses fresh, regional foods and offers a warm, laid-back ambiance. Seasonal items on the menu include beef tartare, apple cobbler, and pumpkin risotto. Additionally well-known for its great coffee and tea assortment is Kohvik Sesoon.

Price range: €10-€20

12. Leib Resto & Aed

In Tallinn's Old Town, there is a well-known restaurant called Leib Resto & Aed. Modern Estonian cuisine is the restaurant's area of expertise, and a focus is placed on utilizing fresh, regional ingredients. The menu offers items like black bread, ice cream, mushroom soup, and smoked pig belly. Additionally, the restaurant includes a garden where they cultivate herbs and vegetables to utilize in their cuisine.

Price range: €20-€40

13. Pegasus

In the center of Tallinn's Old Town, there is a traditional Estonian eatery called Pegasus. Since it first opened in 1964, the eatery has been a local favorite and is still serving traditional Estonian food. Pea soup, black pudding, and herring salad are just a few of the items on the menu that use local, fresh ingredients.

Price range: €15-€30

14 Kaks Kokka

High-end dining establishment Kaks Kokka can be found in Tallinn's hip Rotermann Quarter. Modern Estonian cuisine is the restaurant's area of expertise, and a focus is placed on utilizing fresh, regional ingredients. The menu offers wonderfully presented meals such as wild hog, smoked eel, and elk tartare. The restaurant also offers a wide selection of top-notch Estonian wines on its large wine list.

Price range: €40-€70

15. Must Puudel

In the center of Tallinn's Old Town, you may find the eccentric café and bar Must Puudel. The wallpaper and furnishings at the café are from the past. The menu offers a selection of foods produced with fresh, regional ingredients, such as sandwiches, salads, and cakes. Additionally, Must Puudel offers a wide variety of liquors and beers.

Price range: €5-€15

16. Kaja Pizza Köök & Baar

In the hip Kalamaja neighborhood of Tallinn, there is a casual pizza restaurant called Kaja Pizza Köök & Baar. The eatery is laid down and emphasizes seasonal, regional foods. The pizza selection on the menu includes vegetarian and vegan choices. Craft beers are also abundant at Kaja Pizza Köök & Baar.

Price range: €10-€20

17. Põhjaka Mõis

In a central Estonian manor home that has been reconstructed from the 18th century, Phjaka Mis offers a distinctive dining experience. Known for its farm-to-table philosophy, the restaurant uses a lot of ingredients from the manor's gardens and neighboring farms in its recipes. The menu offers exquisitely presented meals such as beef tartare, smoked salmon, and duck breast. The restaurant also offers a wide selection of top-notch Estonian wines on its large wine list.

Price range: €30-€60

18. Kivi Paber Käärid

In the middle of Tallinn's Old Town stands the hip eatery Kivi Paber Käärid. With an open kitchen and an emphasis on utilizing fresh, local foods, the restaurant offers a simple aesthetic. The menu offers elegantly presented meals, including roasted cauliflower, beef cheek, and apple sorbet. The wine list at Kivi Paber Käärid is likewise good and offers a wide variety of intriguing and uncommon options.

Price range: €20-€40

19. Rukis

In the center of Tallinn's Old Town, you can find the well-known bakery and café Rukis. Traditional Estonian breads, such as rye bread and black bread, are the bakery's specialty. Additionally, the café offers a selection of pastries, salads, and sandwiches, all of which are produced using local, fresh ingredients. The ideal location for a quick lunch or snack while seeing the Old Town is Rukis.

Price range: €5-€15

20. Väike Rataskaevu 16

The well-known Rataskaevu 16 restaurant, which is situated in the center of Tallinn's Old Town, has a casual offshoot called Väike Rataskaevu 16. The menu offers a selection of traditional Estonian dishes produced with fresh, regional ingredients, such as pea soup, black pudding, and herring salad. With both indoor and outdoor seating, Väike Rataskaevu 16 offers a laid-back vibe.

Price range: €10-€20

21. August

The Old Town of Tallinn is home to the upscale restaurant August. The restaurant's design is chic and opulent and places an emphasis on utilizing seasonal, regional foods. The menu offers elegantly presented delicacies, including grilled octopus, roasted duck breast, and elderflower panna cotta. A large selection of top-notch Estonian wines is offered on August's vast wine list.

Price range: €40-€70

22. Patarei Kohvik

On the outskirts of Tallinn, there is a remarkable café called Patarei Kohvik that is housed in a former Soviet jail. With exposed brick walls and a combination of old and contemporary furnishings, the café has an eccentric and eerie aesthetic. Burgers, salads, and sandwiches are just a few of the foods on the menu that are all crafted using fresh, regional ingredients. Additionally, Patarei Kohvik offers a wide variety of artisan beers and beverages.
Price range: €10-€20

23. Kadriorg Kitchen & Bar

In Tallinn's picturesque Kadriorg neighborhood, there is a contemporary restaurant called Kadriorg Kitchen & Bar. The eatery uses a lot of fresh, regional foods and has a trendy, modern atmosphere. The menu offers elegantly presented delicacies such as smoked salmon, mushroom risotto, and rhubarb tart. Additionally, Kadriorg Kitchen & Bar offers a wide selection of top-notch Estonian wines on its large wine list.
Price range: €20-€40

Conclusion

For every taste and price range, Tallinn has a vast selection of eating establishments. There is something for everyone in this fascinating and lovely city, whether you like foreign cuisine or traditional Estonian food. The restaurants and cafés in Tallinn take pleasure in utilizing fresh, regional ingredients to make excellent and memorable meals, from affordable street cuisine to upscale fine dining.

Restaurants like Olde Hansa, Vanaema Juures, and Restoran Peppersack are excellent choices for traditional Estonian food. Visit eateries like NOA and Phjaka Mis for a sample of contemporary Estonian food.

Tallinn offers several alternatives if you're in the mood for foreign food. Delicious pasta dishes are available in Italian restaurants like Trattoria del Gallo Nero and Controvento, while French cuisine is served at establishments like Rataskaevu 16 and August.

Street food establishments like Kompressor, F-Hoone, and Rukis provide delectable and inexpensive lunches for individuals on a tight budget. Restaurants like Tchaikovsky, NOA Chef's Hall, and August are perfect for a special event or a nice night out.

Overall, Tallinn boasts a wide range of restaurants to accommodate every taste and price range. There is something for everyone in this attractive and lovely city, whether you want traditional Estonian food or something a little more cosmopolitan. Prices might vary widely depending on the restaurant, but they are well worth it because of the high quality of the cuisine and the enjoyable eating experience.

Some Advice for Dining Out in Tallinn

- Make a reservation: Many of Tallinn's well-known eateries may become quite full, particularly during the busiest travel season. It's usually a good idea to book a reservation in advance to prevent disappointment.

- Keep an eye out for lunch deals: Many of Tallinn's restaurants offer lunch specials throughout the week, which is a terrific chance to sample some of the regional food without breaking the bank.

- Sample the regional specialties: While visiting Tallinn, make sure to sample some of the regional delicacies. Estonian food is distinctive and delectable. There are several delectable foods to choose from, including smoked salmon, black bread, and sauerkraut.

- Bring cash: Even though the majority of restaurants in Tallinn take credit cards, it's always a good idea to have some on hand, particularly if you're eating at a more formal or informal venue.

- Don't forget the beverages: While visiting Tallinn, sample some of the regional beers since Estonia has a growing craft beer culture. Do not be hesitant to experiment with different foods and beverages since the nation also produces some superb wines and spirits.

Conclusion

Tallinn is a food lover's heaven, with a vast range of restaurants to suit every preference and price range. Everyone may find something they like in this lovely and picturesque city, whether they prefer foreign cuisine or traditional Estonian food. You will undoubtedly find something to satisfy your needs, whether you're searching for a quick snack or a fine dining experience. You won't be disappointed, so go ahead and discover Tallinn's gastronomic treasures!

It's vital to keep in mind that the costs are estimations and might change depending on the menu items, the location, and the time of day. Checking restaurant websites for updated menus and pricing is also a smart idea.

Overall, Tallinn is a foodie's dream, with a wide range of cuisines and eating options to fit every preference and price range. Therefore, be sure to include Tallinn on your list of culinary locations whether you like traditional Estonian food or wish to experience cosmopolitan delicacies.

CHAPTER 5: DAY TRIPS FROM TALLINN: EXPLORING ESTONIA'S COUNTRYSIDE AND COASTAL TOWNS

Estonia's capital, Tallinn, is a quaint medieval city with much to offer. However, if you'd want to escape the city for the day and explore Estonia's countryside and coastal villages, there are plenty of options. In this chapter, we'll discuss some top-day excursions from Tallinn, their costs, and what to anticipate.

1. Lahemaa National Park

With a total size of almost 700 square kilometers, Lahemaa National Park is Estonia's biggest national park. The park is home to a vast diversity of flora and animals and many historic manors and fishing villages. The Palmse Manor House, the Sagadi Manor House, and the Altja Fishing Village are a few of the park's features. You may go biking or hiking on any of the numerous routes that weave through the park. Whether you choose a guided tour or want to go alone, the price of a day trip to Lahemaa National Park might vary, but you should budget between €30 and €50 per person.

2. Pärnu

About 130 km southwest of Tallinn lies the gorgeous beach town of Pärnu. The community is well-known for its stunning sandy beaches, old wooden buildings, and exciting summer festivities. The Pärnu Museum, strolling along the seaside promenade, and having a meal or drink at one of the numerous cafés and restaurants in the town center are just a few of the top things to do in Pärnu. Depending on your travel, a day trip to Pärnu might cost between €20 and €30 for a round-way bus ticket.

3. Tartu

The second-largest city in Estonia is Tartu, 160 kilometers southeast of Tallinn. The city is renowned for its thriving student scene, illustrious university, and lovely Old Town. The Tartu Botanical Gardens, the Town Hall Square, and the University of Tartu Museum are just a few of the highlights of a visit to Tartu. Depending on how you choose to travel, a day trip to Tartu might cost anywhere between €20 and €30 for a round-way bus ticket.

4. Saaremaa

The biggest island in Estonia is Saaremaa, situated off its western coast. The island is renowned for its distinct culture, stunning natural surroundings, and historical sites. Some of the most enjoyable activities in Saaremaa include visiting Kuressaare Castle, exploring the Kaali Meteorite Crater Field, and hiking in Vilsandi National Park. You may anticipate spending between €50 and €100 per person for a day trip to Saaremaa, depending on whether you go for a guided tour or independent exploration.

5. Haapsalu

A lovely seaside village called Haapsalu can be found around 100 kilometers south of Tallinn. The town is renowned for its gorgeous beachfront promenade, historical wooden buildings, and tranquil baths. Visit the Haapsalu Castle, stroll down the Promenade, and unwind in one of the town's numerous spas and wellness facilities are just a few of the best things to do in Haapsalu. Depending on your travel, a day trip to Haapsalu might cost between €20 and €30 for a round-way bus ticket.

6. Viljandi

A little village called Viljandi is roughly 120 kilometers southeast of Tallinn. Its main attractions are the town's picturesque lake, magnificent castle remains, and thriving music scene. Viljandi is known for many great things, including its castle ruins, its lake, and the many music events it holds each year. Depending on your travel, a day trip to Viljandi might cost between €20 and €30 for a round-way bus ticket.

7. Käsmu

A little seaside community called Käsmu is around 80 kilometers northeast of Tallinn. The community is renowned for its stunning coastline views, classic wooden buildings, and extensive maritime history. The Käsmu Maritime Museum, a stroll along the shore, and a tour of the village's characteristic wooden homes are a few of the top things to do in Käsmu. Whether you take a guided tour or want to explore on your own, the price of a day trip to Käsmu might vary, but you should budget between €30 and €50 per person.

8. Otepää

Approximately 190 kilometers southeast of Tallinn lies the little village of Otepää. The community is well-known for its stunning natural scenery, old churches, and winter sports. Visiting the Otepää St. Mary's Church, climbing or skiing in the nearby hills, and taking in the sights at Pühajärve Beach and Park are just a few of the top things to do in Otepää. Depending on how you choose to travel, the cost of a day trip to Otepää might vary but plan to spend between €20 and €30 for a round-way bus ticket.

Conclusion

There are several day trip choices from Tallinn, whether you want to see the breathtaking countryside of Estonia or stop by one of its quaint coastline villages. Each location provides a distinctive experience, from trekking in Lahemaa National Park to unwinding at Haapsalu's spas. Each day trip has a different price depending on other costs like transportation. If you decide to go on a guided tour with little research and preparation, you can easily discover a day trip within your spending limit. So why not escape the city and discover Tallinn's breathtaking surroundings?

The Various Costs Associated With Visiting Estonia's Coastal Towns And Countryside

There are several approaches to discovering Estonia's rural areas and coastal cities, each with special benefits and expenses. Here are some further options for visiting these locations, along with the approximate expenses for each.

1. Cycling Tours

Since cycling tours enable you to cover more land than walking tours while still allowing you to take in the beauty at a leisurely pace, they are a common option for tourists to visit Estonia's rural areas and coastal cities. The Lahemaa National Park and the seaside resort of Haapsalu are just two of the stunning settings in Estonia that you may see on one of the many guided cycling trips available.

A guided bike trip may cost between €50 and €100 per person per day, depending on the duration of the journey and the quality of assistance offered. This price often covers renting a bike, lodging, food, and transportation.

2. Self-Drive Tours

A self-drive trip may be the best choice if you want to explore at your own leisure. Driving through Estonia's countryside and seaside cities is simple, and there are a variety of picturesque roads to choose from. The Haapsalu-Rohuküla coastal route, the Tartu-Kuressaare route, and the coastal routes between Tallinn and Pärnu are a few well-known self-drive routes.

Depending on the trip's duration and the vehicle used, a self-drive tour may cost anywhere between €50 and €100 per day for a modest car. While many inexpensive choices are available in the countryside and seaside towns, this amount does not include lodging or food.

3. Horseback Riding Tours

Consider taking a horseback riding trip to see Estonia's countryside in a really unique manner. Many organizations provide escorted horseback riding excursions through Estonia's most stunning natural settings, including the Lahemaa National Park's woodlands and the Otepää region's undulating hills.

Expect to spend between €50 and €100 per person per day for a guided horseback riding excursion, depending on the duration of the tour and the degree of assistance offered. This price often includes transportation, lodging, food, and horse hire.

4. Kayaking and Canoeing Tours

A kayaking or canoeing excursion could be the best choice if you want to see Estonia's coastal villages from the sea. It is possible to join various guided trips that take you through Estonia's stunning coastal waterways, including the Pärnu River and the area around Haapsalu.

A guided kayaking or canoeing excursion may cost between €50 and €100 per person per day, depending on the duration of the tour and the degree of assistance offered. This price often includes transportation, lodging, food, and equipment rental.

5. Guided Tours

A guided tour may be the way to go if you'd prefer to avoid organizing your trip. Numerous businesses provide guided tours of Estonia's rural areas and coastal cities, including walking bus and boat trips.

Expect to spend between €50 and €100 per person per day for a guided trip, depending on the duration of the excursion and the degree of assistance offered. This price often covers lodging, food, transportation, and tours to nearby sights.

6. Camping

Consider camping as a low-cost option to discover Estonia's countryside. In Lahemaa National Park alone, there are several campsites where you may pitch a tent and spend the night among the wilds of Estonia.

Expect to spend between €10 and €20 per night while camping. However, prices might vary based on the campground and services offered. Meals and equipment rental are not included at this price. However, Estonia has many reasonably priced food stores and places to rent equipment.

7. Walking Tours

Estonia's countryside and seaside towns may be explored leisurely while taking in the landscape and discovering the local history and culture on walking tours. Tallinn, Tartu, and Pärnu are just a few of the towns and cities in Estonia that provide escorted walking tours.

Expect to spend between €20 and €50 per person on each tour for a guided walking tour, depending on the duration of the trip and the degree of assistance offered. This price often includes a guided tour of nearby landmarks and tourist attractions.

8. Public Transportation

Public transportation is a practical and cost-effective choice if you like to explore Estonia's rural areas and seaside cities freely. Estonia has a vast bus and rail network that connects the nation's cities, towns, and villages.

Expect to spend between €5 and €20 for a one-way bus or train ticket, while the price of public transportation might vary based on the route taken and the form of transportation. Accommodations and food are not included with this price. However, there are many reasonably priced choices available all around Estonia.

Generally speaking, depending on your desired means of transportation and degree of assistance, the cost of seeing Estonia's rural areas and seaside cities might vary greatly. Estonia is a great choice for tourists on a tight budget since so many economical choices are available. Estonia is a place that shouldn't be missed because of its breathtaking natural beauty, extensive history, vibrant culture, and kind population.

CHAPTER 6: TALLINN ON A BUDGET: HOW TO EXPERIENCE THE CITY WITHOUT BREAKING THE BANK

The capital of Estonia, Tallinn, is a lovely and pleasant city with a wide variety of attractions for tourists to enjoy. There are many ways to explore Tallinn without going overboard, despite the fact that it might be an expensive trip. We'll look at some of the greatest ways to have fun in Tallinn on a budget in this guide.

1. Free Walking Tours

A walking tour is one of the greatest methods to learn about Tallinn. Fortunately, the city offers a number of free walking excursions. These excursions are guided by experienced and vivacious experts who will show you the city's top sights and impart fascinating historical and cultural knowledge.

The Tallinn Free Tour, which leaves from the Viru Gates in the Old Town every day, is one of the most well-liked free walking tours. The trip includes stops at the Town Hall

Square, Alexander Nevsky Cathedral, and Toompea Castle, as well as other important Old Town attractions. Although gratuities are not required, and the tour is completely free, it lasts around two hours.

2. Explore the Old Town

One of the best-preserved medieval cities in Europe is Tallinn's Old Town, a UNESCO World Heritage site. Due to its small size, the Old Town is simple to navigate on foot. There are a lot of little meandering lanes filled with colorful architecture, stunning cathedrals, and charming stores and eateries.

You can see and do a lot in the Old Town without spending any money. You may stroll around the city walls and take in the scenery, see the churches, or just stroll through the streets and take it all in. The Old Town's hub and ideal area to people-watch are Town Hall Square, so be sure to visit there.

3. Visit Kadriorg Park

A gorgeous park called Kadriorg Park may be found a short distance from the city's heart. The Kadriorg Palace, which Peter the Great erected for his wife Catherine I, can be found in the park. The Estonian Art Museum is presently located in the palace.

The park offers a number of additional attractions outside the palace, such as a lovely Swan Pond, a number of museums, and a Japanese garden. The park is a great place to while away a few hours while taking in the stunning surroundings and serene ambiance.

The park is free to visit, although there is a nominal admission charge for the museums.

4. Visit the Estonian Open Air Museum

On the outskirts of Tallinn, there is an outdoor museum called the Estonian Open Air Museum. The 72-hectare-sized museum includes 14 farms from various parts of Estonia, together with a church, a schoolhouse, and a windmill.

The museum is open for visitors to explore, where they may discover traditional Estonian culture. Traditional skills like weaving and blacksmithing are also shown.

Adult admission to the museum is 8 euros, while a student and senior admission is just 6 euros. Although it is always open, the museum's hours may change according to the time of year.

5. Enjoy the Beach

Despite not being the first spot that comes to mind when considering a beach vacation, Tallinn is home to a number of beaches that are ideal for a day in the sun.

Tallinn's Pirita Beach is the city's most well-liked beach. It is close to the city limits and is readily reached by bus. There are several amenities available at the large, sandy beach, including restaurants, showers, and changing areas.

In Tallinn, Stroomi Beach is another well-liked beach. It is situated in the northern region of the city and is conveniently close to bus stops. Despite being smaller than Pirita Beach, the beach is still a wonderful spot to unwind and soak up the sun.

The use of various amenities may incur a minor cost. However, entry to both beaches is free.

6. Visit the Kumu Art Museum

The Kumu Art Museum is Estonia's biggest and most outstanding art gallery. Aside from its significant collection of Estonian art from the 18th century to the present day, the museum also exhibits both permanent and temporary shows of international art.

The museum is located in an impressive new building. The museum's collection of multimedia displays and interactive exhibits adds a new dimension to the learning experience.

Adult admission to the museum is 14 euros, while a student and senior admission is just 8 euros. Children under the age of eight are admitted free of charge.

7. Try Estonian Cuisine

Although eating out in Tallinn might be pricey, there are many places to sample Estonian food without going over budget. Look for neighborhood bakeries and cafés that provide typical Estonian fares like sauerkraut, potato pancakes, and black bread.

Pea soup with smoked pork is one of Estonia's most well-liked traditional foods. For a fair price, you can get this meal in a lot of neighborhood eateries. Remember to sample some of the regional brews and liqueurs, such as the sweet liqueur Vana Tallinn, which is created with rum and vanilla.

8. Take the Ferry to Helsinki

Take a day trip to Helsinki if you have more time and money to spare. The boat from Tallinn to the Finnish capital takes only two hours, and it often runs all day.

Helsinki is a lovely city that is worthwhile to visit, even for a day. You may visit the city's many museums and art galleries, browse the streets and take in the ambiance, or go to the well-known Market Square.

The boat voyage is a wonderful experience in and of itself, with breathtaking views of the Baltic Sea and the nearby islands. Depending on the season, round-trip boat fares start at around 20 euros per person.

9. Visit the Estonian History Museum

The Estonian History Museum is a great resource for learning about the intriguing history of the nation. The Great Guild Hall, a stunning old structure in the center of Old Town, houses the museum. The exhibit spans the history of the nation from its ancient origins to the present.

Four categories—Land and People, Power and Faith, Daily Life and Entertainment, and The 20th Century—are included in the museum's permanent display. A number of transient exhibits also examine different facets of Estonian history and culture.

The Estonian History Museum charges an 8-euro adult entry price and a 6-euro cost for students and pensioners. Children under the age of eight are admitted free of charge.

10. Go to a Concert or Festival

A lot of concerts and festivals are held all year long in Tallinn, which boasts a thriving music and cultural scene. Many of these events are cost-free or very expensive to attend. To find out what's happening while you're there, look at the neighborhood events calendar.

Tallinn Music Week and the Jazzkaar Festival are two of the city's most well-known music events. A wide range of regional and international artists are included at both events.

11. Take a Day Trip to Lahemaa National Park

Just outside of Tallinn lies the stunning natural reserve known as Lahemaa National Park. The park, which has a surface area of 725 square kilometers, is home to a wide variety of plants and animals. Visitors may discover the park's natural splendor on a number of hiking and nature paths.

A number of old manors and fishing communities that provide a window into Estonia's history are also found in the park. The Palmse Manor House, the Sagadi Manor House, and the Viru Bog are among the park's most well-liked attractions.

Renting a vehicle or joining a tour is the best method to see Lahemaa National Park. Starting at around 20 euros per day, automobile rentals are reasonably priced. Local tour companies provide guided tours, which start at around 50 euros per person.

12. Explore the Kadriorg Palace and Park

Peter the Great constructed the stunning historic estate known as Kadriorg Palace and Park at the beginning of the 18th century. The palace and park are conveniently close to the city's core and are accessible through public transportation.

The park is a well-liked location for outdoor activities, including strolls and picnics. The Kadriorg Art Museum, which exhibits a collection of foreign art from the 16th to the 20th century, is one of the city's many museums and galleries.

Adult admission to the Kadriorg Art Museum is 6 euros, while a student and senior admission is just 3 euros. There is no cost to enter the park.

13. Visit the Seaplane Harbor Museum

In a former seaplane hangar, the Seaplane Harbor Museum is a distinctive maritime attraction. The museum has a variety of antique aircraft, vessels, and submarines, in addition to engaging displays that teach visitors about Estonia's naval past.

The Lembit submarine, which was constructed in the 1930s and used by the Estonian Navy until the 1970s, is one of the museum's attractions. Inside the submarine, visitors may experience what life was like for the crew.

The entrance charge to the Seaplane Harbor Museum is 10 euros for seniors and students and 15 euros for adults. Children under the age of eight are admitted free of charge.

14. Try Some Estonian Cuisine

Estonian food is a unique fusion of traditional foods and contemporary additions. Sauerkraut, smoked salmon and black bread are a few of the meals you must taste. In Tallinn, there are several eateries that provide inexpensive real Estonian food.

The Balti Jaam Market is among the greatest locations to sample cuisine from Estonia. The market, which is close to the Old Town, has a large selection of regional and international culinary choices. Everything is available, including handcrafted shops, street cuisine, fresh vegetables, and baked goodies.

15. Take a Walk in the Kalamaja District

An up-and-coming district called Kalamaja is close to the city's core. The area is renowned for its street art, chic cafés, and bars, as well as its vibrant wooden buildings—a pleasant spot to wander and become acquainted with the neighborhood.

One of the district's characteristics is the Telliskivi Creative City, a repurposed industrial complex that serves as a cultural hub. The complex has a weekly flea market in addition to its many shops, restaurants, and art galleries.

16. Visit the Open-Air Museum

A special attraction that provides a look into Estonia's rural past is the Open-Air Museum. The 72-hectare-sized museum is situated on the outskirts of Tallinn. More than 70 historical structures that were moved there from different locations in Estonia and put back together there may be found there.

Visitors may learn about Estonia's traditional way of life by exploring the farmhouses, windmills, and village stores. Visitors may also see several workshops and demonstrations where traditional crafts and trades are being practiced.

The Open-Air Museum's entrance price is 6 euros for seniors and students and 8 euros for adults. Children under the age of eight are admitted free of charge.

17. Rent a Bike

The best way to experience Tallinn's sights, sounds, and smells while breathing fresh air is by bicycle. The city has several places to hire bicycles at affordable rates.

The Tallinn Coastal Route, which follows the Gulf of Finland and provides breathtaking views of the sea and the city skyline, is one of the most well-known cycling routes. Seventeen kilometers long and takes around 1.5 hours to complete the route.

Starting at around 10 euros per day, bicycle rentals are reasonably priced.

18. Visit the Tallinn Botanic Garden

On the outskirts of the city, there lies a lovely sanctuary called the Tallinn Botanic Garden. The 110-hectare park is home to a varied array of plants and flowers from Estonia and other countries.

The Japanese Garden, the Rose Garden, and the Herb Garden are just a few of the themed gardens that guests may visit. A greenhouse with a variety of tropical plants and flowers is also there.

The Tallinn Botanic Garden charges an adult entry cost of 5 euros and a student and senior access fee of 2 euros. Children under the age of seven may enter for free.

19. Take a Free Walking Tour

The best way to see Tallinn's Old Town without paying any money is on a free walking tour. Local experts who are informed about the city's history and culture lead the excursions.

The Tallinn Free Tour and the Tallinn Alternative Tour are two businesses that provide free walking tours around Tallinn. The excursions normally run for two to three hours and include the most important Old Town sites and attractions. At the conclusion of the trip, give the guide a tip. Typically, 5–10 euros per person should be left as a gratuity.

20. Explore the City's Parks

There are several lovely parks in Tallinn that are ideal for a leisurely walk or a picnic. One of the most well-known parks is Kadriorg Park, which can be found just to the east of the city center. The Kadriorg Palace and the Kumu Art Museum are only two of the historic structures that can be found inside the 70-acre park.

The Pirita Promenade, which provides breathtaking views of the Gulf of Finland, and the Stroomi Beach Park, which is situated in the Kalamaja neighborhood, are two other parks that are well worth seeing.

21. Visit the KGB Museum

An intriguing sight that provides a window into Estonia's Soviet history is the KGB Museum. Previously a top-secret KGB headquarters, the museum is housed in the Hotel Viru's basement.

The different displays may be explored by visitors who want to learn more about the KGB's operations in Estonia during the Soviet period. The KGB Museum charges an adult entry cost of 12 euros and a student or senior admission fee of 10.

22. Attend a Concert or Event

Tallinn has a thriving cultural scene, and there are many performances and events happening all year round. There are events for everyone, from rock festivals to performances of classical music.

The Tallinn Music Week, which takes place in the spring and comprises hundreds of local and international musicians playing in venues all throughout the city, is one of the most well-liked occasions. The Tallinn Black Nights Film Festival and the Jazzkaar International Jazz Festival are two additional well-liked occasions.

Ticket prices vary based on the event and the location.

23. Visit the TV Tower

For everyone interested in panoramic vistas, the Tallinn TV Tower is a must-see site. The tower, Tallinn's highest building, provides breathtaking 360-degree views of the city and its surroundings.

The observation deck is accessible via elevator and is 170 meters above the ground. Additionally, there is a revolving restaurant where you can enjoy panoramic views while you eat.

The Tallinn TV Tower charges an adult entry price of 15 euros and a student or senior admission cost of 10 euros.

24. Take a Day Trip to Lahemaa National Park

One of Estonia's most stunning natural attractions is the Lahemaa National Park, which is situated immediately to the east of Tallinn. There are several hiking paths, waterfalls, and historical attractions inside the 725-square-kilometer park.

Wildlife like moose and lynx may be seen when hiking the numerous routes. The Käsmu Maritime Museum and Palmse Manor are two more old manor residences and fishing communities that are well worth seeing.

Lahemaa National Park is best explored by automobile or by taking a trip with a guide. A guided tour typically costs roughly 30 euros per person.

25. Enjoy Tallinn's Nightlife

There are many pubs and clubs to select from in Tallinn, which boasts a thriving nightlife culture. While the Kalamaja neighborhood has a more contemporary and fashionable vibe, the Old Town is home to some classic taverns and wine bars.

The Studio and Club Hollywood are two of Tallinn's most well-liked nightclubs. There are also a number of places where live music is performed, such as the Von Krahl Theatre and the Rock Cafe.

Depending on the location, entry and drink prices change.

26. Visit the Tallinn City Museum

The Tallinn City Museum is a fantastic resource for learning about Tallinn's past and its inhabitants. The museum features a number of displays that span many eras in Tallinn's history, from the Middle Ages to the Present.

The Tallinn City Museum charges an 8 euro adult entry price and a 6 euro senior and student one.

27. Explore the Seaplane Harbour Museum

The Kalamaja neighborhood's Seaplane Harbour Museum is home to a number of storied ships and aircraft. The displays may be explored by visitors who want to learn more about Estonia's maritime past.

The entrance charge at the Seaplane Harbour Museum is 10 euros for seniors and students and 15 euros for adults.

28. Take a Walk Along the City Walls

The city walls of Tallinn are among the finest preserved in all of Europe and a wonderful area to stroll and take in the scenery. The 13th-century walls provide breathtaking views of the Old Town and the sea.

Visitors may climb many towers around the walls for even greater views. For adults, there is a 5 euro entrance charge, while for students and elderly, there is a 3 euro cost.

29. Visit the Estonian Open-Air Museum

To discover more about Estonia's rural past, visit the Estonian Open-Air Museum, which is nearby Tallinn. Visitors may tour a number of historic structures at the museum, including farms, windmills, and a church.

Visitors may also participate in a variety of traditional crafts and activities, including weaving and blacksmithing.

The Estonian Open-Air Museum's entrance fee is 7 euros for seniors and students and 10 euros for adults.

30. Take a Bike Tour

There are several bike excursions available, and biking is a terrific way to see Tallinn. Tourists have the option of renting bikes and pedaling about the city on their own or joining a guided tour led by locals.

The Old Town Cycling Tour and the Kalamaja Bike Tour are two of the most well-liked cycling tours. A bike tour's price varies according to its length and nature.

31. Visit the Estonian National Opera

One of Estonia's most esteemed cultural organizations, the Estonian National Opera presents a variety of operas, ballets, and concerts every year. The opera theater itself is a stunning old structure that is worth seeing.

Depending on the show and the seat, different prices apply to tickets for the Estonian National Opera.

32. Explore the Estonian Art Museum

The Kadriorg neighborhood's Estonian Art Museum hosts a number of exhibitions that highlight Estonian art from the 18th century to the present day. Throughout the year, the museum hosts a number of foreign exhibits.

The Estonian Art Museum charges an 8 euro adult entry price and a 6 euro senior and student one.

33. Visit the Niguliste Museum

The Old Town's Niguliste Museum is where you can find a number of altarpieces and other works from the Middle Ages. A collection of musical instruments from the 17th century is also housed at the museum.

Adult admission to the Niguliste Museum is 6 euros, while students and pensioners pay just 4 euros.

34. Take a Cooking Class

Several culinary lessons that provide an in-depth understanding of Estonian cookery are offered. Estonian cuisine is a fusion of Scandinavian, Russian, and German influences.

After learning how to prepare traditional foods like black bread and marinated herring, guests may have a lovely feast. A cooking class's price varies according to its kind and length.

35. Visit the Telliskivi Creative City

In the hip Kalamaja neighborhood, there is a center for creativity and innovation called Telliskivi Creative City. A terrific site to discover and absorb the local culture, the region is home to a number of art galleries, design studios, and eateries.

36. Enjoy a Free Walking Tour

In Tallinn, there are a number of free walking tours that are a fantastic opportunity to see the city and discover its history. The Old Town Tour, the Soviet Tour, and the Alternative Tour are a few of the most well-liked walking excursions.

Despite the fact that the tours are free, it is usual to pay the guide a little gratuity at the conclusion of the trip.

37. Explore the Rocca-al-Mare Open-Air Museum

In the vicinity of Tallinn, at the Rocca-al-Mare Open-Air Museum, you may learn a lot about rural life in Estonia in the 18th and 19th centuries. Visitors may tour a number of historic structures at the museum, including farms, windmills, and a schoolhouse.

Visitors may also participate in a variety of traditional crafts and activities, such as weaving and spinning.

The entrance charge to the Rocca-al-Mare Open-Air Museum is 6 euros for seniors and students and 8 euros for adults.

38. Visit the Kadriorg Palace and Park

In the Kadriorg neighborhood, there is a lovely park called the Kadriorg Palace and Park. The Kadriorg Palace, which was constructed by Peter the Great, is one of the historic structures that can be seen in the park.

Visitors may visit the park and the palace while discovering the region's history. Adult entry to the palace is 6 euros, while a student and senior access costs 4 euros.

39. Explore the Patarei Prison

In the Kalamaja neighborhood, there is an old jail called Patarei Jail. Built-in the nineteenth century, the jail remained operational until the 2000s. Visitors may examine the cells and learn about the jail's past since the prison has been converted into a museum today.

The Patarei Prison's entrance cost is 5 euros for adults and 3 euros for youth and seniors.

40. Visit the Lennusadam Seaplane Harbour

A marine museum may be found in the Kalamaja neighborhood near the Lennusadam Seaplane Harbour. Visitors may examine numerous vintage ships and aircraft at the museum to learn more about Estonia's maritime heritage.

Lennusadam Seaplane Harbour entrance is 15 euros for adults and 10 euros for youth and seniors.

Final Thoughts

There are many alternatives for vacationing on a tight budget in Tallinn. Free walking tours, seeing the Old Town, and visiting parks, museums, and beaches are just a few examples of the numerous inexpensive activities and attractions available. You can take advantage of all Tallinn has to offer without going over budget with a little forward preparation and research.

Tallinn is a lovely city that provides the ideal blend of ancient history and technology. It is a well-known travel destination that draws tourists from all over the globe. There are many ways to see Tallinn without going overboard, even if it is not recognized as a cheap city to visit. We'll look at some more strategies to save costs when visiting Tallinn in this post.

CHAPTER 7: TALLINN FOR FAMILIES: FUN ACTIVITIES AND ATTRACTIONS FOR KIDS AND PARENTS ALIKE

Families seeking an exciting vacation can consider visiting Tallinn, the capital of Estonia. Tallinn has lots to offer for guests of all ages, with a variety of historical sites, contemporary conveniences, and outdoor activities. In this guide, we'll detail some of the best family-friendly venues and outings in Tallinn, as well as the prices at which they may be enjoyed.

1. Visit the Old Town

Tallinn's Old Town is one of the best-preserved medieval towns in Europe and a UNESCO World Heritage Site. The Old Town is a fascinating destination to explore with kids because of its meandering cobblestone lanes, vibrant architecture, and old churches. There are many sights and activities to enjoy in the Old Town, such as ascending to the Town Hall in Tallinn for sweeping views of the city, going to the Alexander Nevsky Cathedral, and strolling along the Town Wall.

The Tallinn Town Hall Tower admission fee is €5 for adults and €3 for kids (ages 7 to 18). The Town Wall and the Alexander Nevsky Cathedral may both be seen without charge.

2. Visit the Estonian Open Air Museum

A living museum that depicts typical rural life in Estonia from the 18th to the 20th century is the Estonian Open Air Museum. Visitors may tour the museum's churches, windmills, and farmhouses and even see ancient crafts like weaving and blacksmithing being practiced. The museum also holds yearly festivals and monthly activities.

The Estonian Open Air Museum admission fee is €8 for adults and €5 for kids (ages 7 to 18).

3. Take a Tallinn Card City Tour

The Old Town, Kadriorg Park, and Pirita Beach are just a few of the city's top sights that may be seen on the hop-on, hop-off Tallinn Card City Tour. The trip, which departs every 30 minutes and has an audio guide in eight different languages, makes it simple to visit all of Tallinn's best attractions quickly.

Tallinn Card City Tours are available for a 24-hour price of €22 for adults and €11 for kids (ages 7 to 18). Kids under the age of seven ride free.

4. Explore the Tallinn Zoo

More than 13,000 animals from 548 different species may be seen in the Tallinn Zoo. Everything from polar bears and penguins to elephants and giraffes is available for visitors to observe. The zoo also has a children's playground and a petting zoo.

Tallinn Zoo admission is €12 for adults and €8 for kids (ages 3 to 17). Infants and toddlers are admitted for free.

5. Visit the Seaplane Harbour Museum

A former seaplane hangar now serves as the home of the maritime museum Seaplane Harbour. A steam icebreaker and a submarine are among the vintage ships and boats that may be seen by visitors. Children may explore a submarine, control a ship, and don sailor costumes in interactive exhibitions.

Adults must pay €15 to enter the Seaplane Harbour Museum; minors (ages 7 to 18) must pay €8. Under-7s are admitted free of charge.

6. Go Ice Skating

Tallinn features a number of outdoor ice skating rinks in the winter, one of which is in Town Hall Square in the Old Town. The entire family may enjoy this simple and enjoyable pastime since skates can be rented on-site.

Price: Depending on the rink, ice skating in Tallinn costs between €3 and €5 for kids and €5 to €7 for adults.

7. Enjoy Tallinn's Parks and Beaches

There are several parks and beaches in Tallinn that are great for a picnic or a day in the sun. Kadriorg Park is a popular destination for families since it is conveniently located near the heart of the city. The park has a stunning palace, a number of museums, and a sizable body of water where guests may hire paddle boats. Pirita Beach is a well-liked location for beachgoers, featuring a lengthy stretch of sandy beach and a number of coastal eateries.

Entry to Kadriorg Park is free. However, paddle boat rentals at the pond cost €6 per hour. Pirita Beach does not charge admission, although parking may be an additional cost.

8. Visit the Tallinn TV Tower

With a height of 314 meters, the Tallinn TV Tower is the highest structure in Estonia. Visitors may use a fast elevator to get to the tower's top level, where they can take in expansive views of the city and its surroundings. A hands-on exhibit about Estonian TV and radio broadcasting history is also housed in the tower.

Entry to the Tallinn TV Tower is priced at €14 for adults and €8 for kids (ages 7 to 18). Under-7s are admitted free of charge.

9. Visit the NUKU Theatre and Museum

A puppet theater and museum, NUKU Theatre and Museum present Estonia's history and puppetry culture. Visitors may see a puppet performance, engage in a workshop to learn how to construct their own puppet, or just view the collection of marionettes and puppets on exhibit.

Entry to the NUKU Theatre and Museum is priced at €8 for adults and €5 for kids (ages 3 to 18). Infants and toddlers are admitted for free.

10. Go on a Tallinn Food Tour

Tallinn is a food lover's heaven, offering both traditional Estonian fare and contemporary fusion cuisine. Families may have fun trying new cuisines while learning about the city's culinary heritage by taking a food tour. There are several businesses that provide culinary excursions, with choices including Old Town walking tours and bike tours of the suburbs.

Price: Food tours range in price from €30 to €70 per person, depending on the operator and the duration of the trip.

11. Visit the Estonian Open Air Museum

In the Rocca al Mare neighborhood of Tallinn, there is an outdoor museum called the Estonian Open Air Museum. With more than 70 structures from various parts of Estonia, the museum depicts traditional village life in Estonia. Visitors may take part in seminars and activities, learn about traditional crafts, and observe farm animals.

The Estonian Open Air Museum admission fee is €15 for adults and €10 for kids (ages 7 to 18). Under-7s are admitted free of charge.

12. Explore the Seaplane Harbour

In the Port of Tallinn, there is a maritime museum called Seaplane Harbour. Along with interactive displays and simulators, the museum has a variety of vintage ships, submarines, and seaplanes. Additionally, visitors may participate in a variety of seminars and activities as well as a guided tour of the museum.

Adults must pay €16 to enter the Seaplane Harbour, while minors (ages 7 to 18) must pay €10. Under-7s are admitted free of charge.

13. Take a Tallinn City Tour

Families may visit Tallinn and discover the city's history and culture by taking a city tour. There are several businesses that provide city tours, with choices ranging from bus excursions of the suburbs to walking tours of the Old Town. Some trips may include stops at well-known landmarks like Kadriorg Park or the Tallinn TV Tower.

Price: The cost of a city tour varies based on the provider and the duration of the trip, but it normally costs between €10 and €50 per person.

14. Visit the Kumu Art Museum

The biggest museum of art in Estonia is the Kumu Art Museum, which is situated in the Kadriorg neighborhood of Tallinn. Along with worldwide contemporary art, the museum has a collection of Estonian artwork from the 18th century to the present. The museum also holds several events, activities, and seminars throughout the year.

Price: Adults must pay €10 to enter the Kumu Art Museum; minors (8 to 18) must pay €5. Under-8s are admitted free of charge.

15. Take a Day Trip to Lahemaa National Park

Just south of Tallinn, the stunning Lahemaa National Park is a natural area with a number of hiking routes, historical monuments, and scenic attractions. In addition to historic Estonian towns and manor homes, visitors may witness bogs, coastal cliffs, and waterfalls. Additionally, a number of activities and guided tours are offered, such as cycling, canoeing, and wildlife viewing.

Lahemaa National Park doesn't charge admission, although parking may cost extra. Depending on the operator and the activity, guided tours and activities might cost anywhere from €20 and €50 per person.

16. Visit the Tallinn Zoo

The Tallinn Zoo, located in the Rocca al Mare district, is home to around 8,000 species from all over the globe. There are various endangered species, as well as tigers, elephants, and giraffes, that visitors may observe. The zoo also offers a kids' zoo, a playground, and different year-round activities and events.

The Tallinn Zoo admission fee is €15 for adults and €8 for kids (ages 3 to 17). Infants and toddlers are admitted for free.

17. Visit St. Olaf's Church

One of Tallinn's most recognizable landmarks is the medieval St. Olaf's Church, which is situated in the city's Old Town. The tower of the church, which was once the highest edifice in the world, is open to the public so they may enjoy spectacular views of the city from above.

St. Olaf's Church admission is €5 for adults and €2 for kids (ages 7 to 18). Under-7s are admitted free of charge. Please be aware that those with mobility concerns or a fear of heights shouldn't climb the tower.

18. Take a Food Tour of Tallinn

Tallinn is renowned for its delectable cuisine and distinctive culinary customs. Families can go on a food tour of the city and try regional specialties like marzipan, smoked fish, and black bread. Food tours are provided by a number of businesses, and options include everything from

Old Town walking tours to excursions to nearby markets and eateries.

Price: Food tours range in price from €30 to €70 per person, depending on the operator and the duration of the trip.

19. Visit the Estonian Health Museum

Families can learn about the human body and health in a fun and interactive way at the Estonian Health Museum, which is located in Tallinn's Old Town. In addition to participating in a variety of interactive games and activities, visitors can explore exhibits on anatomy, nutrition, and disease prevention.

The Estonian Health Museum admission fee is €8 for adults and €5 for kids (ages 7 to 18). Under-7s are admitted free of charge.

20. Take a Ferry to Helsinki

Families may board a boat from Helsinki to Tallinn for a delightful day excursion since the two cities are only separated by the Gulf of Finland. Visitors may enjoy Helsinki's various sites, including the Suomenlinna Fortress, the Helsinki Cathedral, and the Market Square, during the quick 2-hour boat voyage.

Price: Prices for ferry tickets vary based on the business and the time of year but normally range from €20-€50 per person.

Conclusion

Tallinn is a terrific location for families, providing a range of fun and instructive activities for all ages. This beautiful Baltic city has something for everyone, from sightseeing in the Old Town's historical sites to learning about Estonian culture and traditions at museums and attractions.

The pricing stated for each activity is current as of May 2023 and is subject to change. It is advised that tourists check the websites of each attraction or activity for up-to-date prices and hours of operation before visiting.

Whether you're traveling for a weekend or a longer stay, Tallinn is guaranteed to surprise and inspire families searching for a great holiday.

Overall, Tallinn provides a broad choice of exciting activities and attractions for families to enjoy, from touring the Old Town to visiting museums and parks. With rates that are relatively reasonable compared to other European locations, Tallinn is an excellent alternative for families searching for a budget-friendly trip.

CHAPTER 8: NIGHTLIFE IN TALLINN: THE BEST BARS, CLUBS, AND VENUES TO CHECK OUT AFTER DARK

Estonia's capital, Tallinn, is a dynamic city with a booming nightlife. In this vibrant city, there is something for everyone, from upscale rooftop bars to subterranean clubs. This guide will examine the top Tallinn pubs, clubs, and places to visit after dark.

1. Pudel Baar

The quaint and relaxed pub Pudel Baar is situated in the hip Kalamaja district. Along with a limited range of wines and drinks, the bar offers a wide variety of craft beers from Estonia and throughout the globe. The casual and warm ambiance makes it a fantastic place to start your night out.

Price: Beers start at around €3.50

2. Must Puudel

Must Puudel, which is also in Kalamaja, is a well-liked destination for both residents and tourists. The bar's unusual design, which includes old furniture and a jumble of decorations, gives it a distinctive and inviting atmosphere. DJs perform a wide variety of music, from techno to independent rock. A small dance floor is also available for individuals who would want to get their groove on.

Cocktails start at around €8.

3. Hell Hunt

One of Tallinn's oldest and most well-known bars, Hell Hunt, has been operating since 1993. The tavern offers a warm, traditional atmosphere thanks to its rustic decor, which includes exposed brick walls and wooden beams. A modest menu of traditional Estonian cuisine is available at Hell Hunt, along with a wonderful range of beverages, including their own house brew.

Beers start at around €3 in price.

4. F-Hoone

A hip restaurant and bar called F-Hoone is housed in an old industrial structure in Kalamaja. High ceilings and big windows in the contemporary, industrial interior give it a roomy, open vibe. The menu combines cuisine from Estonia and other countries, and the bar provides a wide range of wines, beers, and cocktails.

Cocktails start at around €9, while entrees cost between €15 and €20.

5. NOP

In Tallinn's Old Town, there is a stylish and contemporary pub called NOP. The bar's stylish décor, which includes marble countertops and soft velvet seats, gives it a posh and refined appearance. A variety of drinks, wines, and spirits are available on the menu, along with a few foods prepared in the tapas manner.

Cocktails start at around €10 in price.

6. Butterfly Lounge

On the rooftop of the Swissotel Tallinn, there is a chic and sophisticated bar called Butterfly Lounge. The bar is a terrific place to watch the sunset or have a drink late at night since it provides breathtaking views of the city. A variety of wines and beverages are available on the menu, along with a limited number of appetizers.

Cocktails start at around €15.

7. Club Hollywood

One of Tallinn's largest and most well-liked nightclubs is called Club Hollywood. Each of the club's several rooms has a unique theme and musical genre, ranging from hip-hop to EDM. As a result of the dynamic and energizing ambiance, it's a terrific place to dance the night away.

Admission fees range, with beverages starting at around €5.

8. Studio

In the center of Tallinn's Old Town stands Studio, a small yet energetic nightclub. The club plays a variety of house and techno music and has an excellent sound system. It's a terrific place to go out with friends because of the cozy and welcoming ambiance.

Admission fees range, with beverages starting at around €5.

9. Sinilind

The traditional Estonian tavern Sinilind is situated in the hip Kalamaja district. The inside of the tavern is classic, with wooden paneling and antique furnishings giving it a warm, homey atmosphere. With friends, Sinilind is a terrific place to unwind with a few beers and sample some authentic Estonian cuisine.

Beers start at around €3 in price.

10. Club Studio

The renowned nightclub Club Studio is situated in downtown Tallinn. The club features a variety of rooms, each with its own musical genre, from pop to electronic dance music. As a result of the dynamic and energizing ambiance, it's a terrific place to dance the night away.

Admission fees range, with beverages starting at around €5.

11. The Clazz

In the center of Tallinn's Old Town, The Clazz is a chic and elegant jazz club. The club boasts a stylish design with velvet chairs and dim lighting that give it a posh and cozy atmosphere. Of course, the music is jazz, and both local and foreign performers often play there.

Admission fees range, with refreshments starting at around €8.

12. Von Krahl

In the center of Tallinn's Old Town, Von Krahl is a well-known theater, bar, and nightclub. The room has a distinctive and lively air thanks to the varied and unusual furnishings and décor. There are frequent concerts and events in the pub, which also offers a fantastic assortment of beers and beverages.

Admission fees range, with beverages starting at around €5.

13. Sessel Salong

In the hip Kalamaja district, there is a quaint and small cocktail bar called Sessel Salong. The bar's stylish and contemporary décor, together with the low lighting and plush couches, make it a fantastic place for a quiet drink with friends or a romantic evening out. A variety of spirits and cocktails, as well as a few small appetizers, are available on the menu.

Cocktails start at around €12 per serving.

14. Club Privé

High-end nightclub Club Privé is situated in the center of Tallinn's Old Town. With soft seats and beautiful furnishings, the club's opulent and sophisticated atmosphere exudes exclusivity and glamour. House and techno are mixed together in the music, and foreign DJs often play there.

Admission fees range, with beverages starting at around €10.

15. Kompressor

In the center of Tallinn's Old Town, Kompressor is a well-known tavern. Huge pancakes with a variety of sweet and savory fillings are the pub's specialty. It's a terrific place to unwind with some substantial meals and a few drinks because of the interior's old furnishings and wooden paneling.

Price: Beers start at around €3, pancakes at about €5.

Conclusion

From quaint pubs to upscale nightclubs, Tallinn's nightlife culture has plenty to offer for everyone. In this vibrant and diverse metropolis, you may find everything from a quiet night with friends to a wild night on the town. There are alternatives for any budget. However, prices vary based on the institution.

CHAPTER 9: EXPLORING TALLINN'S CULTURAL SCENE: MUSEUMS, GALLERIES, AND PERFORMING ARTS VENUES

The cultural and artistic center of Estonia is Tallinn. The city is well-known for its extensive past, distinctive architecture, and thriving cultural life. Tallinn has a variety of museums, art galleries, and performance spaces, so it has something to offer everyone interested in discovering its cultural side. We'll examine some of Tallinn's top cultural sites in further detail in this post to see what they have to offer.

Museums:

Tallinn is home to a variety of museums that serve a variety of interests. You may discover a museum that appeals to you, whether your interests are history, art, science, or technology. The following are a few of Tallinn's best museums:

1. Estonian National Museum - One of the biggest museums in the nation, the Estonian National

Museum provides a look into Estonian history and culture. The museum has a noteworthy collection of artifacts, records, and images that highlight the nation's rich cultural legacy. Adult admission is priced at 14, while student and senior admission is priced at 7.

2. Kumu Art Museum - The biggest museum in Estonia, the Kumu Art Museum exhibits both modern and traditional artwork from Estonia and other nations. Multimedia installations, sculptures, and paintings are all part of the museum's collection. Adult admission is priced at 14, while student and senior admission is priced at 7.

3. Seaplane Harbor - Located among Tallinn's historic seaplane hangars, the Seaplane Harbor is a maritime museum. The museum displays a variety of ships, from steamboats to submarines, as well as Estonia's nautical history. Adult admission is 15 euros; students and seniors pay 8 euros.

There are several additional significant museums in Tallinn in addition to the three museums already listed. One of these is the Museum of Occupation, which documents the nation's history of tyranny and occupation during the Nazi and Soviet regimes. The museum has displays that examine both the effects of occupation on Estonian culture and society as well as the lives of common Estonians during these turbulent years. Adult admission to the Museum of Occupation is 6 euros, while student and senior admission is just 3 euros.

The Estonian History Museum, which depicts Estonia's history via a variety of exhibits and relics, is another fascinating museum in Tallinn. The museum has displays on Estonian folklore, medieval history, and the nation's freedom fight. The Great Guild Hall, the Maarjamäe Palace, and the Viru Hotel KGB Museum are just a few of the Tallinn locations of the Estonian History Museum. The cost of admission varies according on the branch and the on-view exhibits.

Galleries:

If you like art, Tallinn has a variety of galleries that feature both domestic and foreign works. The following are a few of Tallinn's best art galleries:

1. Temnikova & Kasela Gallery - Temnikova & Kasela Gallery is one of Estonia's top galleries for modern art. The gallery hosts exhibits by local and foreign artists, presenting anything from sculpture to painting. Free entry is offered.

2. Draakon Gallery - Showcasing modern Estonian art, Draakon Gallery is one of Tallinn's oldest galleries. A variety of media, from painting to installation, are included in the gallery's solo and group shows. Free entry is offered.

3. ArtDepoo Gallery - Situated in the center of Tallinn, ArtDepoo Gallery exhibits modern art. The gallery hosts exhibits by local and foreign artists, presenting anything from painting to photography. Free entry is offered.

There are several additional art galleries in Tallinn that are worthwhile seeing in addition to the three previously listed ones. The Niguliste Museum and the Kadriorg Art Museum are two of its many locations in the city. Another one of them is the Art Museum of Estonia. A variety of exhibits showing Estonian art from the 18th century to the current day are available at the Art Museum of Estonia. Adult admission to the Art Museum of Estonia is 12 euros, while student and senior admission is just 6 euros.

The Kai Art Center is a contemporary art space in Tallinn that presents exhibits, performances, and events that examine the relationship between art, technology, and society. The Kai Art Center specializes on experimental and multidisciplinary art and exhibits works by regional and worldwide artists. The Kai Art Center has no entrance fees.

Performing Arts Venues:

Along with having a variety of theaters, concert halls, and opera houses, Tallinn also boasts a thriving performing arts scene. The following are a few of Tallinn's best performance spaces:

1. Estonia Theatre - One of Estonia's oldest theaters, Estonia Theatre presents a variety of theatrical performances, from opera to drama. Concerts and other cultural events are also held in the theater. The cost of tickets varies according on the show.

2. Nordea Concert Hall - The biggest concert venue in Estonia, Nordea Concert Hall presents a variety of classical and modern music events. Theater and dance acts are also held in the concert hall. The cost of tickets varies according on the show.

3. Kanuti Gildi SAAL - Showcasing experimental and avant-garde acts, Kanuti Gildi SAAL is a modern performing arts venue. The center presents performers from across the world as well as local talent, displaying everything from dance to drama. The cost of tickets varies according on the show.

Tallinn boasts a number of other theaters and music halls in addition to the three performing arts centers already listed that are worth seeing. One of them is the Russian Theater, which presents plays and musicals in Russian. Over a century has passed since the Russian Theater first became a focal point of Russian cultural life in Tallinn. Depending on the show, the cost of tickets for the Russian Theater varies.

The Kanuti Gildi SAAL Studio, a smaller, more secluded theatre that presents experimental and avant-garde performances, is another intriguing location. Focused on multidisciplinary works that straddle the lines of theater, dance, and performance art is the Kanuti Gildi SAAL Studio. Depending on the performance, Kanuti Gildi SAAL Studio ticket rates change.

Cultural Events:

Tallinn presents a number of cultural events all year round in addition to the usual programming at museums, galleries, and performance spaces. The Tallinn Old Town Days, which take place in the summer and honor the city's rich history and cultural legacy, are one of the most well-liked occasions. Numerous activities, like as concerts, street performances, and historical reenactments, are presented during the Tallinn Old Town Days.

The Tallinn Christmas Market, which takes place in the Old Town throughout the holiday season, is another well-liked occasion. The Tallinn Christmas Market offers holiday decorations, local food and drink, and a variety of cultural activities, such as choir concerts and a Santa Claus appearance.

Conclusion

There are several museums, galleries, and performance spaces in Tallinn that may accommodate a variety of interests and preferences. There is something for everyone in Tallinn, from discovering the rich history and culture of Estonia to attending contemporary art exhibitions and musical concerts. It is worthwhile to take the time to explore Tallinn's cultural scene whether you are a native or a tourist to the city.

While some of Tallinn's cultural sites are free to enter, others charge a fee. The cost of entry varies, although most art galleries and museums provide discounts to children and the elderly. It's also important to keep in mind that certain locations could provide free entry on particular days or at particular hours.

Tallinn also holds a variety of cultural events throughout the year, including as music festivals, art exhibits, and theatrical performances, in addition to museums, galleries, and performing arts centers. Tallinn Music Week, Tallinn Black Nights Film Festival, and Tallinn Photomonth are a few of the city's most well-liked events.

Tallinn has a thriving and varied cultural environment, with a variety of museums, galleries, and performance spaces that highlight the city's rich history and creative talents. While some of Tallinn's cultural sites have an entrance cost, many of them give students and seniors discounts, and other places even let people in for free on particular days or at certain hours. In addition, Tallinn offers a number of cultural occasions all year long, including as music festivals, art shows, and theatrical productions.

Discovering Tallinn's cultural scene is amusing as well as educational. By visiting the city's museums, tourists may learn more about Estonia's history and cultural heritage, while art enthusiasts can peruse the galleries to see the creations of national and international artists. Live performances provide a variety of shows to enjoy, from experimental theater to traditional folk music.

Additionally, the cultural scene in Tallinn is essential to the city's tourist sector. The Estonian Tourist Board reports that due to the country's vibrant contemporary arts scene and rich cultural legacy, cultural tourism is one of the country's fastest-growing subsectors of the tourist business.

When compared to other European cities, Tallinn's cultural attractions are often more reasonably priced. Smaller art galleries and theaters often have lower entrance prices than some of the bigger museums and performing arts centers. In addition, many of Tallinn's cultural events provide free or inexpensive entry.

Finally, discovering Tallinn's cultural scene is a must-do experience for tourists. Tallinn provides a variety of possibilities to explore its history, art, and cultural legacy via its museums, galleries, performing arts centers, as well as a range of cultural events held throughout the year. Make sure to take the time to explore Tallinn's cultural offerings, whether you have a few hours or a few days to spare.

CHAPTER 10: ACTIVE ADVENTURES IN TALLINN: HIKING, BIKING, AND WATER SPORTS IN AND AROUND THE CITY

Tallinn, the capital of Estonia, is well-known for its outdoor activities in addition to its attractive old town and lovely architecture. The city provides a variety of physical activities to suit all interests and fitness levels. Tallinn provides activities for everyone, whether you're an adrenaline addict or just looking for some downtime. Here are some of the greatest outdoor things to do in and around Tallinn, including bicycling, hiking, and more.

Hiking in and around Tallinn:

1. Toompea Hill: Toompea Hill is a must-see for all hikers and is situated in the center of Tallinn's ancient town. The city and its surroundings may be seen from this peak in all directions. You may begin your journey from the base of the hill and go to the summit to take in the breathtaking views. The ascent takes around 30 minutes and is a short trek.

2. Pirita Promenade: For a leisurely trek, this five km-long promenade is ideal. The Pirita River promenade provides stunning views of the sea and the Tallinn skyline. At the end of the promenade lie the remains of the Pirita Convent, which you may also explore.

3. Keila-Joa Park: Keila-Joa Park is a great destination for a day trek and is just 30 minutes from Tallinn. A number of routes in the park go through the forest, beside the Keila River, and ultimately to the Keila-Joa Waterfall. The park's entry price is €3 per person, and it is open all year round.

Biking in and around Tallinn:

1. Kadriorg Park: This park is among the most gorgeous sites in Tallinn to go riding. Biking pathways in the park lead you through the gardens, woodlands, and all around the Kadriorg Palace. At the park's entrance, bicycle rentals are available for €8 per hour.

2. Kopliranna Seikluspark: Just 10 minutes from the heart of Tallinn, this adventure park provides a variety of outdoor pursuits, including mountain biking. The park has a number of paths with varied

degrees of difficulty, and you can hire a mountain bike there for €12 an hour.

3. Viimsi Nature Trail: Viimsi Nature Trail is a great destination for a family bike trip and is just 20 minutes from Tallinn. Along with passing through the woodland, the walk follows the Viimsi coastline. From the trailhead, you may hire a bike for €5 an hour.

Water Sports in and around Tallinn:

1. Tallinn Bay: Tallinn Bay is a great place to go kayaking, paddleboarding, or sailing. The Tallinn Bay Surf Center offers hourly kayak and paddleboard rentals for €10.

2. Pirita Beach: Kiteboarding and windsurfing are popular activities at Pirita Beach. You may hire equipment from the beach for €25 per hour and enjoy these activities in optimum wind conditions.

3. Prangli Island: This undiscovered treasure lies just off the coast of Tallinn and provides a variety of water sports activities, including fishing, scuba diving, and snorkeling. For €50 per person, you may book a guided excursion from Tallinn to Prangli Island.

Other outdoor adventures in and around Tallinn:

1. Rocca al Mare Adventure Park: Just 15 minutes from the heart of Tallinn, Rocca al Mare Adventure Park is the ideal setting for an active day of outdoor recreation. The park has a range of sports, such as paintball, rope climbing, and zip-lining. The park has a €20 per person entrance charge, and the cost of the various activities varies.

2. Lahemaa National Park: This park is ideal for a day excursion and is situated approximately an hour's drive from Tallinn. The park provides a variety of outdoor activities, such as canoeing, biking, and hiking. For €75 per person, you may book a guided journey from Tallinn to Lahemaa National Park.

3. Aegna Island: Aegna Island, which lies just off the coast of Tallinn, is an excellent destination for a day excursion. Hiking, riding, and swimming are just a few of the outdoor activities available on the island. For €10 per person, you may take a ferry from Tallinn to Aegna Island.

Depending on the activity, the location, and the time of year, Tallinn's outdoor activity costs might change. However, the majority of activities are inexpensive, making them available to everyone. It is always advised to verify rates and availability before making a reservation.

In summary, Tallinn is an excellent vacation spot for outdoor lovers. The city provides a variety of outdoor excursions that are suitable for all levels of fitness and interests, thanks to its attractive old town and gorgeous natural surroundings. Tallinn offers a variety of activities for all interests, including riding, hiking, and water sports. Get outside and see all this lovely city has to offer!

There are a ton of additional experiences in and around Tallinn in addition to the outdoor pursuits described above. Options like bungee jumping and skydiving are available for those looking for an experience that is more adrenaline-inducing. In the adjacent town of Pärnu, you may go bungee jumping, where you can leap 50 meters from a bridge above the Pärnu River. The Estonian Aviation Academy offers skydiving, where you may jump out of an aircraft at 3,000 meters and enjoy the rush of freefalling before your parachute deploys. These activities range in price but typically cost between $50 and $100 per person.

Horseback riding and golf are two possibilities for those seeking a more leisurely trip. You may take guided trips through the woods and countryside at one of the several horseback riding facilities in and around Tallinn. There are various golf courses in the city where you may play, including the top-rated Niitvälja Golf Course in Estonia. Expect to spend between €50 and €100 per person for horseback riding and between €50 and €150 per person for golfing, depending on the particular activity.

Visit the Patarei Prison Museum if you want an uncommon and off-the-beaten-path experience. The cells, interrogation halls, and execution chamber of this old Soviet jail may all be seen within the museum that has been created there. It's an eerie, interesting event that sheds light on Estonia's past as a Soviet satellite. It costs €6 per person to enter.

Last but not least, no trip to Tallinn would be complete without taking in the historical and architectural splendor of the city. Numerous medieval churches, town halls, and merchant homes may be seen in the old town, which is a UNESCO World Heritage Site. You may learn about the city's history and architecture by taking a guided walking tour of the old town. However, the cost of these trips varies, budget between €10 and €20 per person.

Overall, Tallinn provides a broad selection of outdoor sports and experiences to suit all tastes and fitness levels. There is something for everyone in this lovely city, whether you want an exhilarating adventure or a quiet day out.

What are you still holding out for? Get outside and begin your explorations!

CHAPTER 11: WHERE TO STAY IN TALLINN: FROM LUXURY HOTELS TO BUDGET HOSTELS AND APARTMENTS

Estonia's capital city, Tallinn, is a fascinating blend of contemporary elegance and old-world charm. The city is a popular destination for both leisure and business visitors because of its rich history, lively culture, and thriving economy. Finding the ideal lodging is crucial whether you're traveling to Tallinn for a business trip, a family holiday, or a weekend escape. In this guide, we'll examine some of the top lodging choices in Tallinn, including anything from five-star hotels to affordable hostels and flats.

Luxury Hotels in Tallinn:

1. Hotel Telegraaf

The opulent 5-star Hotel Telegraaf, which is situated in the center of Tallinn's Old Town, provides a fusion of contemporary luxury and traditional grandeur. The hotel is located in a former telegraph office, and the Art Deco façade of the building has been exquisitely preserved. The rooms are spacious and nicely appointed, and they come equipped with all of the amenities that one would anticipate finding in a high-end hotel, like free WiFi, flat-screen televisions, and minibars. In addition, the Hotel Telegraaf has a spa, a gym, and a chic restaurant serving fine dining.

Cost: The Hotel Telegraaf's nightly accommodation prices start at around 200 euros.

2. Swissotel Tallinn

In the center of Tallinn's commercial sector sits the 5-star Swissotel Tallinn. In addition to providing convenient access to the Old Town and other well-known sights, the hotel boasts breathtaking views of the city and the Baltic Sea. The luxurious and roomy accommodations at Swissotel Tallinn have contemporary conveniences like flat-screen TVs, complimentary WiFi, and Nespresso coffee makers. There are a variety of eating choices, a rooftop bar with panoramic views, a spa, and a fitness facility at this hotel.

Cost: The Swissotel Tallinn's nightly accommodation prices start at around 150 euros.

3. Hotel Palace

The 4-star Hotel Palace is located in the heart of Tallinn, only a short walk from the historic district. The hotel's room sizes and suites, which come with flat-screen TVs, minibars, and complimentary WiFi, mix traditional elegance with contemporary comfort. The Hotel Palace also has a restaurant serving modern Estonian cuisine, a spa, and a fitness facility.

Cost: The Hotel Palace's nightly accommodation prices start at around 100 euros.

4. Swissotel Tallinn

In the center of Tallinn's commercial sector sits the opulent 5-star Swissotel Tallinn. The hotel provides opulent and roomy suites with flat-screen TVs, minibars, and complimentary WiFi. The hotel also has a fitness center, an indoor pool, and a spa and wellness area. Several eating choices are available at Swissotel Tallinn, including a fine-dining restaurant, a lobby bar, and a rooftop bar with city views.

Cost: The Swissotel Tallinn's nightly accommodation prices start at around 150 euros.

5. Hilton Tallinn Park

Only a short distance from Tallinn's Old Town lies the opulent 5-star Hilton Tallinn Park. The hotel provides opulent and roomy suites with flat-screen TVs, minibars, and complimentary WiFi. The hotel also has a fitness center, an indoor pool, and a spa and wellness area. Several eating choices are available at Hilton Tallinn Park, including a fine-dining restaurant, a lobby bar, and a rooftop bar with expansive city views.

Cost: The Hilton Tallinn Park's nightly accommodation prices start at around 120 euros.

6. Hotel Telegraaf

In the center of Tallinn's Old Town stands the opulent 5-star Hotel Telegraaf. A large number of the building's original characteristics have been retained at the hotel, which is built in a historic structure that was previously a telegraph office. The hotel provides tasteful, roomy suites with flat-screen TVs, minibars, and complimentary WiFi. The Hotel Telegraaf also has a spa and wellness center, a fitness center, and an indoor pool. Estonian modern cuisine is served at the hotel's restaurant.

Cost: The Hotel Telegraaf's nightly accommodation prices start at around 200 euros.

Mid-Range Hotels in Tallinn:

1. Park Inn by Radisson Meriton Conference & Spa Hotel Tallinn

In the heart of the city, a short stroll from the Old Town lies the 4-star Park Inn by Radisson Meriton Conference & Spa Hotel Tallinn. The hotel offers large, contemporary-styled rooms and suites that are equipped with flat-screen TVs, minibars, and complimentary WiFi. Additionally, the Park Inn by Radisson Meriton Conference & Spa Hotel Tallinn has a spa, a fitness center, and an international restaurant.

Price: The Park Inn by Radisson Meriton Conference & Spa Hotel Tallinn offers rooms starting at around 70 euros per night.

2. Hotel St. Barbara

In the center of Tallinn's Old Town stands the 3-star Hotel St. Barbara. The hotel occupies a building dating back to the 19th century, and as such, it has rooms that are decorated in a classical style. The hotel has a sauna and a restaurant that offers traditional Estonian fare, and the rooms include flat-screen TVs, minibars, and free WiFi.

Cost: The average nightly charge for a room at Hotel St. Barbara is around 50 euros.

3. Original Sokos Hotel Viru

Three-star Original Sokos Hotel Viru is a hotel in the center of Tallinn that is a short stroll from the Old Town. The hotel has a distinguished past being the former tallest structure in Estonia and KGB headquarters during the Soviet period. Since then, the hotel has undergone renovations and now provides cozy and contemporary rooms and suites with flat-screen TVs, minibars, and complimentary WiFi. In addition to a restaurant and a bar, the Original Sokos Hotel Viru has a KGB Museum that provides an intriguing look into the hotel's history.

Cost: The Original Sokos Hotel Viru's nightly accommodation prices start at around 60 euros.

4. Radisson Blu Sky Hotel

In Tallinn's commercial sector, there is a mid-range hotel called the Radisson Blu Sky Hotel. The hotel provides spacious, contemporary rooms and suites with complimentary WiFi, minibars, and flat-screen TVs. The hotel also has a fitness center, an indoor pool, and a spa and wellness area. Several eating choices are available at the Radisson Blu Sky Hotel, including a fine-dining restaurant and a lobby bar.

Cost: The Radisson Blu Sky Hotel offers rooms starting at around 80 euros per night.

5. Park Inn by Radisson Central Tallinn

In the center of Tallinn's Old Town, there is a mid-range hotel called Park Inn by Radisson Central Tallinn. The hotel provides spacious, contemporary rooms and suites with complimentary WiFi, minibars, and flat-screen TVs. The hotel also has a sauna and a fitness facility. The Park Inn by Radisson Central Tallinn has a restaurant and a bar.

Price: Nightly prices at the Park Inn by Radisson Central Tallinn begin at around 60 euros.

6. Tallink City Hotel

In Tallinn's commercial sector sits the mid-range Tallink City Hotel. The hotel provides spacious, contemporary rooms and suites with complimentary WiFi, minibars, and flat-screen TVs. The hotel also has a fitness center, an indoor pool, and a spa and wellness area. There are a number of eating choices available at Tallink City Hotel, including a restaurant, a lobby bar, and a nightclub.

Cost: The Tallink City Hotel's nightly accommodation prices start at around 60 euros.

Budget Hostels and Apartments in Tallinn:

1. Old Town Hostel Alur

In the center of Tallinn's Old Town sits the low-cost hostel known as Old Town Hostel Alur. The hostel provides both private rooms and dormitory-style accommodations, both of which are straightforward and unadorned yet tidy and welcoming. Additionally, the hostel has a kitchen, a common area, and free WiFi.

Cost: A bed in a dormitory room at the Old Town Hostel Alur costs around 10 euros per night.

2. OldHouse Hostel

In the center of Tallinn's Old Town, there is a cheap hostel called OldHouse Hostel. The hostel provides both private rooms and dormitory-style accommodations, both of which are straightforward and unadorned yet tidy and welcoming. Additionally, the hostel has a kitchen, a common area, and free WiFi.

Cost: A bed in a dormitory room at OldHouse Hostel starts at around 15 euros per night.

3. Old Town Central Apartments

If you're on a tight budget and want to stay in the center of Tallinn's Old Town, consider the Old Town Central Apartments. The flats and apartments, which are very basic and straightforward yet tidy and pleasant, are spread out among a number of old structures. A kitchenette, a private toilet, and free WiFi are included in the units.

Cost: A studio apartment in the Old Town Central Apartments starts at around 40 euros per night.

4. Red Emperor Hostel

In the center of Tallinn's commercial sector sits the low-cost hostel known as Red Emperor. The hostel provides a selection of pleasant, hygienic dorm rooms and private rooms. Additionally, the hostel has free WiFi, a lounge space, and a communal kitchen. Budget-conscious tourists seeking a peaceful location can choose the Red Emperor Hostel.

Cost: At Red Emperor Hostel, individual rooms start at around 30 euros per night, while dorm rooms start at about 10 euros.

5. Center Hotel

In the center of Tallinn's Old Town stands the low-cost Center Hotel. The hotel provides cozy, spotless rooms with flat-screen TVs, minibars, and complimentary WiFi. In addition, the Center Hotel has a restaurant and a bar. For tourists on a tight budget looking for a convenient place to stay, the hotel is an excellent choice.

Cost: The Center Hotel's nightly accommodation prices start at around 40 euros.

6. Tallinn Backpackers

In Tallinn's Old Town, there is a cheap hostel called Tallinn Backpackers. The hostel provides a selection of pleasant, hygienic dorm rooms and private rooms. Additionally, the hostel has free WiFi, a lounge space, and a communal kitchen. For tourists on a tight budget looking for a sociable environment to stay in, Tallinn Backpackers is a fantastic choice.

Cost: At Tallinn Backpackers, dorm room prices begin at around 10 euros per night, while private room rates begin at roughly 30 euros per night.

7. Go Hotel Shnelli

A cheap hotel called Go Hotel Shnelli can be found not far from Tallinn's Old Town. The hotel provides cozy, spotless rooms with flat-screen TVs, minibars, and complimentary WiFi. Additionally, Go Hotel Shnelli has a restaurant and a bar. For guests on a tight budget who wish to stay near the Old Town, the hotel is a fantastic choice.

Cost: The Go Hotel Shnelli's nightly accommodation prices start at around 40 euros.

Conclusion

Tallinn has a variety of lodging choices, from opulent 5-star hotels to affordable hostels and flats. Whether you're planning a business trip, a family holiday, or a romantic retreat, Tallinn offers a variety of lodging options to fit every taste and budget. There are many locations to stay in Tallinn that will enable you to see all this dynamic and historic city has to offer, from the picturesque Old Town to the contemporary business sector.

Tallinn has a broad range of lodging alternatives for all price ranges. Tallinn offers accommodations for every price range, from five-star hotels to cheap hostels and flats. Swissotel Tallinn, Hilton Tallinn Park, and Hotel Telegraaf are all excellent choices if you want an opulent place to stay. The Radisson Blu Sky Hotel, Park Inn by Radisson Central Tallinn, and Tallink City Hotel are all excellent options if you're searching for mid-range lodging. In addition, Old Town Hostel Alur, Red Emperor Hostel,

Center Hotel, Tallinn Backpackers, and Go Hotel Shnelli are excellent choices if money is a concern.

Whatever lodging option you choose in Tallinn, you will undoubtedly enjoy your time spent discovering this beautiful and ancient city.

CHAPTER 12: SEASONAL EVENTS IN TALLINN: FESTIVALS, MARKETS, AND CELEBRATIONS THROUGHOUT THE YEAR

Estonia's main city, Tallinn, is a lovely and energetic location with a deep cultural history. The city is renowned for its historical significance, beautiful architecture, and medieval Old Town. Tallinn features a number of seasonal events all year round, including festivals, fairs, and celebrations. In this post, we'll look at some of Tallinn's most well-liked seasonal events, their dates, and what they have to offer tourists.

Spring

After a long winter, spring is a fantastic time to visit Tallinn since the city begins to come to life. The city's parks and gardens begin to blossom with vibrant blooms, providing a stunning background for outdoor festivities despite the sometimes frigid weather.

1. Tallinn Music Week

Popular music event Tallinn Music Week is held in late March or early April. At the event, over 200 performers from Estonia and across the globe will take the stage at different locations throughout the city. Indie, pop, rock, electronic, and other musical genres are among those included at the event. The festival offers a conference for experts in the music business, making it a fantastic venue for networking and education.

Price: A one-day entry to Tallinn Music Week costs around €35.

2. Tallinn Spring Days

In April, Tallinn Spring Days is a festival honoring the arrival of spring. In addition to concerts, seminars, and guided tours of the city's parks and gardens, the festival offers a wide range of other events and activities. In addition to the event, there is a flower market where guests may purchase plants and flowers to take home.

Tallinn, Spring Days activities range in price from free to having a nominal cost for some.

3. Tallinn Old Town Days

Tallinn Old Town Days is a celebration that honors the vibrant cultural legacy of the city and is held in late May or early June. The festival offers a wide range of performances, seminars, guided tours of the city's ancient structures, and marketplaces with a medieval theme. A procession that features traditional Estonian attire and culture is also part of the celebration.

Many of the Tallinn Old Town Days activities are free, while others may charge a nominal fee.

Summer

Tallinn's summer season, when the weather is nice and the days are long, is the busiest. Visitors may enjoy the city's parks and beaches as well as outdoor activities and festivals that bring the city to life.

1. Tallinn Maritime Days

The Tallinn Nautical Days celebration honors the city's nautical history and is held in late May or early June. There are many different events and activities during the festival, including boat excursions, music, seminars, and a seafood market. A ship procession entering the port is another feature of the celebration.

Cost: The majority of the Tallinn Maritime Days activities are free, although some may charge a nominal price.

2. Tallinn Medieval Days

The Tallinn Medieval Days event honors the city's medieval past and is held in the middle of July. The festival offers a wide range of performances, seminars, guided tours of the city's ancient structures, and marketplaces with a medieval theme. Visitors may see knights participate in different tasks during the festival's knight tournament.

Many of the Tallinn Medieval Days activities are free, while others may charge a nominal fee.

3. Tallinn FoodFest

Tallinn FoodFest is a festival that honors the city's culinary sector and is held in the first few days of August. There are many other events and activities during the festival, including culinary classes, tastings, and seminars. In addition to the event, there is a market where guests may purchase regional cuisine and drink items.

Price: Tallinn FoodFest tickets start at around €10.

Autumn

Tallinn is especially lovely in the autumn when the city's parks and trees change hues of gold and crimson. The time of year is ideal for outdoor activities because of the crisp, chilly air.

1. Tallinn Black Nights Film Festival

The renowned Tallinn Black Nights Film Festival, often known as PFF, takes annually every November. Feature films, documentaries, and short films from Estonia and other countries are among the films shown during the festival. For both movie buffs and industry professionals, the festival offers seminars and panel discussions.

Cost: Tallinn Black Nights Film Festival tickets start at around €8.

2. Tallinn Restaurant Week

In October and November, there is a cuisine festival called Tallinn Restaurant Week. At the festival, more than 50 restaurants in Tallinn will be serving cheap prix fixe dinners. Visitors to the event get the chance to sample a variety of local foods and eateries.

For Tallinn Restaurant Week, prix fixe dinners start at around €10.

3. Tallinn Light Festival

An event called the Tallinn Light event happens in late September or early October. Numerous light projects and projections are part of the event, which transforms the city at night into a wonderful place. The festival also offers seminars for people interested in making their own light art, as well as guided tours of the installations.

Numerous Tallinn Light Festival installations and seminars are free to attend.

Winter

As the city's cobblestone streets and old buildings are draped in snow and dazzling lights throughout the winter, it is a lovely time to visit Tallinn. Christmas markets and activities in the city are a must-see this time of year.

1. Tallinn Christmas Market

From late November to early January, the city's Town Hall Square hosts the well-known Tallinn Christmas Market. More than 100 sellers provide handcrafted items, presents, and traditional cuisine and drink from Estonia during the market. A Christmas tree, live musical acts, and a visit from Santa Claus are all included in the market.

Entry to the Tallinn Christmas Market is free, although there are different charges for food and goods.

2. Tallinn Winter Festival

In December and January, there is a celebration called the Tallinn Winter Celebration. The festival offers a wide range of performances by theater companies, concerts, and workshops. The event also features a New Year's Eve celebration with live music and fireworks in the city's Town Hall Square.

Several of the Tallinn Winter Festival's activities are free. However, others may have a nominal price.

3. Tallinn St. Martin's Day Fair

The Tallinn St. Martin's Day Fair honors the conclusion of the harvest season and is held in November. A wide range of merchants offering regional goods, handcrafted items, and traditional Estonian cuisine and drink can be found at the fair. A parade and musical acts are also included during the event.

Price: The Tallinn St. Martin's Day Fair is free to enter. However, there are different charges for food and presents.

Finally, Tallinn provides a broad range of seasonal activities all year round. There is always something going on in Tallinn, from concerts and cuisine festivals to Christmas markets and light festivals. Visitors get a wonderful chance to enjoy the history, gastronomy, and culture of the city during these events. Even while event costs might vary, many are free or just cost a small amount. Tallinn is a charming and exciting city that is well a visit in any season.

CHAPTER 13: DISCOVERING TALLINN'S SOVIET PAST: EXPLORING THE CITY'S HISTORY AND ARCHITECTURE

Estonia's capital, Tallinn, is renowned for its magnificent Old Town and ancient buildings. The city also has an intriguing Soviet heritage that is just waiting to be unearthed. Exploring Tallinn's Soviet history and architecture may provide tourists with a unique and interesting experience, from Soviet-era buildings to tales of life under the Soviet administration. In this paper, we will examine some of the most well-known Soviet-era structures in Tallinn as well as its history.

Estonia was occupied by the Soviet Union beginning in 1940, and the occupation lasted until 1991. Tallinn saw enormous changes throughout this period, affecting both its outward look and its social and political climate. The Soviet government launched a massive urbanization initiative that resulted in the construction of several new structures and public areas.

The Linnahall, a significant music and sporting arena close to the waterfront, is one of Tallinn's most recognizable Soviet-era structures. Soviet architect Raine Karp created the Linnahall, which was constructed in 1980 for the Moscow Olympics. The building is a stunning example of Soviet-era design because of its unusual Brutalist architecture and concrete facade. Even though the Linnahall is no longer in operation, tourists who want to learn more about Tallinn's Soviet history continue to flock there.

The Maarjamäe Palace, which was constructed in the early 20th century and used as a summer palace for the Russian royal family, is another significant site in Tallinn's Soviet past. The palace served as a museum devoted to the history of the Soviet Union during the time of the Soviet Union. The Estonian History Museum, which has exhibits on Estonian history from ancient times to the present, is now housed in the palace.

Another significant example of Soviet-era architecture is seen in the city center at the Tallinn Song Festival Grounds. The 1960-built Song Festival Grounds have hosted several significant historical occasions, notably the 1988 Singing Revolution, which was pivotal in Estonia's fight for independence from the Soviet Union. The grounds are still utilized for cultural events today, and visitors interested in Estonian history and culture often visit them.

Along with these iconic buildings, Tallinn is home to a large number of further specimens of Soviet-era architecture and design. Many elements of the city's urban environment still bear the imprint of the Soviet era, from residential complexes to public spaces.

Visitors may get a unique perspective on the history and culture of Tallinn by investigating the city's Soviet past. Travelers may learn more about Estonia's complex history and the effects of the Soviet occupation by visiting sites like the Linnahall, Maarjamäe Palace, and the Tallinn Song Festival Grounds. It's important to recognize and value Tallinn's extensive and nuanced past as the city develops and becomes more contemporary.

Hearing the accounts of individuals who experienced it is one of the most fascinating parts of learning about Tallinn's Soviet history. Many locals have distinct recollections of life in a nation that was under Soviet control, and their personal stories may provide insightful perspectives into the everyday reality of life in a country that was under Soviet influence.

Visit the KGB Museum, which is housed in the old KGB headquarters in the city center, to learn more about

Tallinn's Soviet past. The exhibit provides a sobering look at the techniques used by the Soviet secret police to keep the Estonian populace under control. Visitors may see displays on the KGB's techniques for surveillance and questioning, as well as the jail cells where political prisoners were housed.

The Museum of Occupations, which explores Estonia's history under Soviet and Nazi control, is another worthwhile museum to visit. The museum showcases both exhibitions on the resistance groups that arose in reaction to the political and cultural persecution that Estonians endured during Soviet control.

Of course, discovering Tallinn's Soviet history involves more than simply seeing monuments and museums. It also involves taking in the distinctive ambiance and culture of the place. For instance, a trip to the neighborhood market may provide a window into life in Tallinn now and during the Soviet period. A glimpse into Tallinn's history and present may be seen in the city's markets, many of which have been in operation for many years.

Finally, learning about Tallinn's Soviet past is a rewarding experience that may give tourists a better grasp of the history and culture of the city. Travelers may get a personal understanding of Estonia's complex history by going to places like the Linnahall, Maarjamäe Palace, and the Tallinn Song Festival Grounds, as well as institutions like the KGB Museum and the Museum of Occupations. The exploration of Tallinn's Soviet past is a remarkable experience, whether you're a history enthusiast or just interested in experiencing the city's distinctive atmosphere.

CHAPTER 14: PLANNING YOUR TRIP TO TALLINN: TIPS ON VISAS, TRANSPORTATION, AND LOCAL CUSTOMS

Estonia's capital city, Tallinn, is a stunning location with a fascinating past and thriving present. Tallinn has something for everyone, whether you want to explore the ancient Old Town, indulge in regional cuisine, or take in the city's nightlife. Here are some pointers on visas, transportation, and local traditions to help you make the most of your vacation to Tallinn.

Visas

You do not need a visa to visit Estonia if you are a citizen of the European Union, Switzerland, or one of the other nations that make up the Schengen Area. Without a visa, you are permitted to remain in the nation for up to 90 days within a 180-day term. You may need a visa to enter Estonia if you are a citizen of a nation outside of the Schengen Zone. To find out whether you need a visa and what the criteria are, visit the website of the Estonian Ministry of Foreign Affairs.

Transportation

Tallinn is accessible by both local and international flights thanks to the city's well-connected airport. It is simple to combine a vacation to Tallinn with other locations in the area because of the ferry links between Tallinn and Helsinki, Stockholm, and St. Petersburg.

There are several alternatives for transportation once you get to Tallinn. The city boasts an effective bus, tram, and trolley public transit system. Tickets may be bought via kiosks or the driver directly. A single ticket costs €2; however, smartcards that provide savings for repeated rides may also be purchased.

In Tallinn, taxis are also commonly accessible. You can either hail one on the street or order a trip using an app. In comparison to other European cities, Tallinn's taxi fares are quite inexpensive, costing an average of €5 to €10 for a short trip.

Tallinn's small size and well-preserved Old Town make it simple to move about on foot if you like to explore the city on foot. Walking is a fantastic method to see the city's stunning buildings and important sites.

Local Customs

The culture of Estonia is distinct, having its own traditions and customs. When visiting Tallinn, bear the following in mind:

Language: Although English is widely used in Tallinn, particularly in tourist areas, Estonian is the official language of the country. Learning a few fundamental words and phrases in the native tongue, such as "Tere" (hello) and "Aitäh" (thank you), is always considered courteous.

In Estonia, it's usual to shake hands while introducing yourself to someone. It's customary for males to shake hands more strongly than women, although matching the other person's grasp is always courteous. It's also typical to give close friends and family members a short embrace or kiss on the cheek.

Eating and Drinking: Hearty, traditional meals from Estonian cuisine include stews, smoked salmon, and black bread. You may find something to suit every taste at Tallinn's many restaurants, many of which also serve foreign food. When dining out, if service is not already included in the bill, it's traditional to leave a tip of around 10%. In Estonia, drinking is a common habit. Tallinn has a vibrant nighttime scene with a wide variety of pubs and clubs.

Punctuality: Being on time for meetings and appointments is crucial since Estonians place a high value on it. It's considerate to phone or leave a message to inform the other person if you're going to be late.

Prices

Tallinn is a reasonably priced vacation spot in comparison to other European towns. However, costs might change based on where you travel and what you do. Here are some examples of average Tallinn pricing for typical expenses:

Accommodations: Tallinn offers a variety of lodging choices, ranging from high-end hotels to hostels that are affordable. Hostel beds may be purchased for as little as €10–€20 per night, whereas a midrange hotel room normally costs between €60 and €100 per night.

Food and Drink: A lunch at a mid-range restaurant in Tallinn typically costs between €15 and €20 per person. Meals in quick food establishments and on the streets start at around €5, making them even more affordable. In a pub or restaurant, a beer will run you around €3–€5, while a glass of wine would set you back about €5–€8.

Transit: While a smart card for several journeys may provide savings, a single public transit ticket costs €2. The usual rate for a short journey in a taxi is between €5 and €10, making them reasonably priced. The city also offers bike rentals, with rates beginning at around €5 per hour.

Attractions: Many of Tallinn's finest sights, including the Old Town and many museums, are open to the public without charge. However, certain excursions and museums may have an entry price. For instance, the Tallinn TV Tower costs adults €13 and children €9.

Tallinn is a fantastic location for vacationers on a tight budget since you can take in the city's rich history and culture without going overboard.

In conclusion, there is a lot to see and do in Tallinn, a fascinating and ancient city. Tallinn has something for everyone, whether you want to explore the ancient Old Town, indulge in regional cuisine, or take in the city's nightlife. You may maximize your journey to this lovely location according to this advice on visas, transportation, and regional traditions.

CONCLUSION

As individuals have become more conscious of how their travel choices affect the environment, society, and local economies, sustainable tourism has gained importance in recent years. Making deliberate decisions to reduce negative consequences while enhancing good ones is essential to sustainable travel. This essay will examine environmentally friendly tourism in Tallinn, Estonia, and provide helpful advice for responsible tourism and community support.

Tallinn's sustainable tourism is a historic city with a distinctive cultural heritage. It serves as the nation's economic hub and Estonia's capital. However, the city's infrastructure, ecology, and local communities are now stressed due to the tourist industry's recent fast rise. In response, the local government has started several programs to encourage ecotourism.

The "Tallinn Card," a city permit that grants visitors access to public transit, museums, and other attractions, is one of the key projects. By encouraging visitors to use the bus or train instead of a cab or a rental vehicle, this card encourages environmentally friendly travel by lowering air pollution and traffic congestion.

The "Green Key" accreditation, given to hotels, hostels, and other lodgings that satisfy certain environmental requirements, is another program. The accreditation covers standards for water conservation, waste reduction, and energy efficiency. Tourists may lessen their personal environmental effects and support environmentally friendly companies by staying in lodgings that have earned the Green Key certification.

Along with these efforts, Tallinn also provides a range of sustainable tourist activities, including outdoor sports like cycling and hiking, as well as guided tours that concentrate on the history and culture of the city. These activities support sustainable travel by offering alternatives to activities that have detrimental environmental or social effects.

Tips for Responsible Tourism in Tallinn

1. Choose Sustainable Accommodations: Seek inns and hostels that have received sustainability certificates, such as the Green Key. This will lessen your personal environmental effect and promote environmentally friendly companies.

2. Use public transportation: The Tallinn Card gives you access to public transportation, so use this choice instead of

getting a car or taking cabs. This will lessen air pollution and traffic congestion.

3. Support Local businesses: When you travel, try to support local companies by dining at neighborhood eateries, buying at neighborhood markets, and taking part in tours and activities run by local tour operators. The local economy and the city's distinctive cultural legacy will benefit from this.

4. Be Mindful of Your Environmental Impact: When you travel, make an effort to have as little of an effect as possible on the environment by saving electricity and water, cutting down on trash, and avoiding single-use plastics. This might be as easy as bringing a reusable water bottle or shutting off the lights and air conditioner when you leave your room.

5. Respect the Local Culture: Respecting the local traditions and culture while visiting a new location is crucial. This might include knowing the language well, dressing correctly, and knowing regional customs and etiquette.

Conclusion

A rising trend in travel is sustainable, which aims to maximize beneficial effects while minimizing negative ones. The Tallinn Card and the Green Key accreditation are two projects that the municipal administration of Tallinn, Estonia, has started to encourage sustainable tourism. You may be a responsible traveler and aid local communities by picking eco-friendly lodging, using the public transit system, supporting neighborhood businesses, being aware of your environmental effect, and respecting local customs.

Printed in Great Britain
by Amazon

26701954R00079